CONTENTS

KW-119-087

Introduction

Money Matters is the seventy-fourth volume in the **Issues** series. The aim of this series is to offer up-to-date information about important issues in our world.

Money Matters examines young people's personal finances and the issue of money management.

The information comes from a wide variety of sources and includes:
Government reports and statistics
Newspaper reports and features
Magazine articles and surveys
Web site material
Literature from lobby groups
and charitable organisations.

It is hoped that, as you read about the many aspects of the issues explored in this book, you will critically evaluate the information presented. It is important that you decide whether you are being presented with facts or opinions. Does the writer give a biased or an unbiased report? If an opinion is being expressed, do you agree with the writer?

Money Matters offers a useful starting-point for those who need convenient access to information about the many issues involved. However, it is only a starting-point. At the back of the book is a list of organisations which you may want to contact for further information.

*****

Wellbeing

Money Matters

ISSUES

Volume 74

Editor

Craig Donnellan

WITHDRAWN

MIDDLESBROUGH LIBRARY
THE NORTHERN SCHOOL ART

Independence

Educational Publishers

B050855

First published by Independence
PO Box 295
Cambridge CB1 3XP
England

© Craig Donnellan 2004

Copyright
This book is sold subject to the condition that it shall not,
by way of trade or otherwise, be lent, resold, hired out or otherwise
circulated in any form of binding or cover other than that in which it
is published without the publisher's prior consent.

Photocopy licence
The material in this book is protected by copyright. However, the
purchaser is free to make multiple copies of particular articles for instructional
purposes for immediate use within the purchasing institution.
Making copies of the entire book is not permitted.

British Library Cataloguing in Publication Data
Money Matters – (Issues Series)
I. Donnellan, Craig II. Series
332'.024055'0941

ISBN 1 86168 263 8

Printed in Great Britain
MWL Print Group Ltd

Typeset by
Claire Boyd

Cover
The illustration on the front cover is by
Pumpkin House.

Catching them young

As personal finances become more complex, so the need for young people to learn about handling money becomes as essential as health and sex education

By Penny Kitchen

Students with money to spare are a rare breed. It is estimated that an average student will expect to owe anything from £7,000 to £10,000 by the time they have completed their university studies.

A frugal lifestyle and a part-time job can't always prevent financial difficulties for the young. Costs of everything from student accommodation to transport have risen and grants have either abolished or drastically reduced. Yet, if students can learn about quantum physics, world economics and the meaning of life, why not about the management of money? Organising money matters can seem difficult and complicated, especially for inexperienced young people with limited resources. But help is available to make it easier.

The Financial Services Authority was set up to act as the public's financial watchdog, but it has also been given the key role of promoting public understanding of the financial system. The thinking behind this is that better-informed consumers will be in a stronger position to manage their personal finances effectively and to protect themselves from buying financial products which don't suit them. 'We see an important part of our strategy as helping people acquire the knowledge, aptitude and skills necessary for becoming questioning and informed consumers of financial services; in short, helping them to go out there and get a fair deal for themselves,' says Kate Bristowe of the FSA. The younger this process of learning begins the better.

A recent MORI poll showed 48 per cent of secondary schoolchildren want to learn more about money than other life skills such as health

or sex. So lessons on money are now in the national curriculum – what it is, where it comes from, where it goes and, crucially, how to manage it. The FSA has prepared teaching resources – such as Mega Money and Colossal Cards – and guidance for teachers on encouraging children to think responsibly about money from an early age. The hope is that this and future generations of schoolchildren reach adulthood financially literate and less likely to get into debt.

Even though some progress is being made, financial mismanagement among young people, especially in higher education, remains a major problem. One study published last year by Bristol University urged schools and colleges to give sixth-formers lessons in money management, in preparation for university 'to reduce the risk of depression and anxiety among debt-ridden students'.

The abolition of grants and their replacement with loans was fostering a 'debt culture' with many students becoming resigned to owing large sums. Many were overusing credit cards and overestimating their earning power after graduation and ability to repay the debt.

Many students had no idea about such things as interest-free overdrafts and low-interest graduate accounts being offered by several high street banks, or by Internet banks such as Egg. Furthermore, many young people are being persuaded into buying merchandise using store cards with attractive '10 per cent off' introductory offers. They realise too late that swingeing APRs lie in store when they fail to pay the card off.

Pension planning is another area where the young are naively optimistic about the future. Less than a fifth of 18- to 24-year-olds who are working say they are members of an occupational scheme and only one in 50, or 2 per cent, have a personal pension plan. Deborah Arnott, FSA's head of Consumer Education Ser-

Income - outgoings - savings = Disposable income

vices, said: 'It is perfectly understandable that the younger you are the less inclined you are to think about retirement savings. But if, as they say, most people want to maintain their standard of living in retirement, they've got to start saving early.'

Antonia Senior, writing in *The Times* last year, gave a graphic example of the principles at work: 'A 23-year-old saving £50 a month would have a pension pot of £100,000 which, on current rates will buy a pension of just £7,500 a year at the age of 65. Waiting until the age of 30 to save the same sum will almost halve the pension pot to £63,000. But how many 23-year-olds earning less than £25,000 a year can afford to spare £50 a month while trying to save the money for a house deposit?' Not many.

Bank account choices

A good place for students to start getting to grips with personal finance is by choosing a bank account that suits their needs. There are two basic types of account: an introductory account (sometimes called a basic or a starter account) and a current account. An introductory account is best if they don't want a cheque book or the risk of becoming overdrawn by mistake. These types of accounts offer straightforward services like a card to draw cash from a 'hole in the wall' or bank branch and a way of paying bills, either by direct debit or standing order. Some introductory accounts also offer a debit card to pay for things in a shop, over the phone or the Internet. Many employers, even of casual and 'Saturday job' workers, are asking for bank account details so that earnings can be paid direct.

If, however, a student wants a cheque book and overdraft facility – bearing in mind that charges and interest will have to be paid on what is owed – then a current account would be a better choice. Current accounts also offer cheque guarantee cards and debit cards. Many banks offer special student deals so it's well worth shopping around.

To help people who want to know more about setting up a bank account, the FSA has recently

More than a PIN number

A major survey in 2001 questioned young people about savings, insurance and pensions. Most aspire to have all three but lack the money.

■ 90 per cent think it is very important to avoid debt, but 50 per cent are currently in debt.

■ 70 per cent think it is important to insure their belongings, but only 10 per cent have such insurance.

■ 90 per cent think they need to start a pension, but only 10 per cent have actually started one.

This overall picture of a responsible attitude combined with a lack of money is reinforced by the way they handle debt. Three-quarters are taking proactive steps to pay their debts off and they shun high-interest money lenders and credit cards in favour of the Government's Social Fund which charges no interest.

Other key findings of the survey include:

The majority agreed they would benefit from financial advice, but only a third had ever received any.

■ The most common way of paying bills is through key/card systems meaning respondents are paying around 25 per cent more for their electricity than billed customers.

■ Cashpoints are widely used, but limited use is made of branches themselves. Use of telephone and Internet banking is very limited.

launched a leaflet *No bank account? Why it could pay you to have one*. It gives the low-down on bank accounts in plain language and highlights how money can be saved by paying bills by direct debit. A website called www.studentmoneynet.co.uk asks you to answer five or six simple questions and then presents specific accounts (or credit cards or loans etc.) matching your needs. Banks, insurance and financial services companies advertise on the site and there are direct links to many of them, but the information provided is free and impartial. There is also information on all aspects of funding student life including details on Government loans and sponsorships.

Very useful checklists outlining the kind of questions that need to be asked are available in the 'Financial Products' section of the FSA's Consumer Help website. It is a resource of easy-to-understand, independent information for anyone wanting simple explanations of different products and financial services. 'Bear in mind, though, that the FSA's role is to increase understanding of financial issues, not to make decisions for people,' says Kate Bristowe. 'So the information on our website will not tell people what to do or try to flog them anything, but it will help them do their homework.'

If the student then wants to compare between companies on other sites, they will have a basic understanding.

Having limited resources means that students need to think carefully about issues like loans, credit and insurance. They need to be warned about the danger inherent in store cards, for instance, and to value their possessions. These days students possess hundreds of pounds' worth of equipment such as mobile phone, stereo and computer, but chances are these are uninsured, a risk not fully appreciated until the worst happens and the items are stolen.

As mothers know well, but many students have yet to discover, the trick to making ends meet is to budget, budget, budget! That simply means balancing what's going out against what's coming in. If spending exceeds income, then the student should look at ways to cut back on spending. Money management is not quantum physics, but it could get your son or daughter's financial life onto an even keel and that is just as important!

■ The above information is from the magazine *Woman's World*, a magazine of the National Federation of Women's Institute.

© *Woman's World*

A generation unskilled in the art of budgeting

One in five callers to the National Debt Line is under 25 and 250,000 of the people who consult Citizens' Advice Bureaux about financial problems each year are under 30

'Credit is a way of life to this generation,' says Carl Bayliss of National Debt Line, which helps people sort out their debt problems. 'It's easily available and can be useful, but only when used responsibly.'

Two-thirds of the problems younger people have with debt is related to credit cards, store cards, overdrafts, loans and other sorts of easy credit, he says. 'Budgeting is a life skill but many children never learn how to handle it.'

Much concern has been voiced about student debt. But, while graduates now expect to leave university with debts of about £10,000 each, the evidence suggests that students are better able to cope with their debts than other young people.

Far from spending wildly, credit cards represent only two per cent of the average student's debt when leaving university, according to research by Barclaycard. More than 90 per cent of students with Barclaycards are classified as having a 'good' credit rating, meaning they manage their credit more effectively than the average cardholder.

In contrast, while most 15- and 16-year-olds questioned in a recent NOP survey knew how much a computer game costs, they were unsure how to budget for food, rent and bills. Few had any idea of costs when it came to heating, lighting, rent and council tax.

More than a quarter (26 per cent) believed that, when they moved out of home, one of their three biggest expenses would be going out, while 24 per cent thought they would spend most on clothes – and one in five thought the biggest expense would be their mobile phone bill.

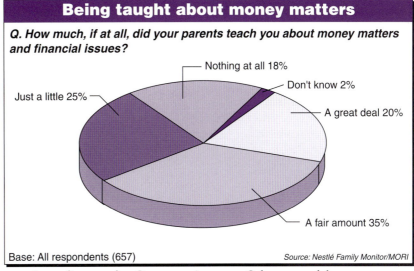

Being taught about money matters

Q. How much, if at all, did your parents teach you about money matters and financial issues?

- Nothing at all 18%
- Don't know 2%
- A great deal 20%
- Just a little 25%
- A fair amount 35%

Base: All respondents (657) — Source: Nestlé Family Monitor/MORI

According to the Consumers' Association, more than 6m families find it difficult to repay their debts. 'The only feasible way of providing access to advice on pensions and debt and helping to deliver educational initiatives effectively, is to establish a National Financial Advice Network to complement private sector capacity,' a spokesman says.

'We strongly support the principle of financial education and think the FSA should devote more resources to it. However, given the legacy of problems in the UK, any educational initiatives would be slow-burning. Until the effects have fed through to the general population, we see no substitute for unbiased, consumer-focused financial advice.'

When people get into debts, many have no idea of the best way to tackle the problem, he says. Although free help is available from Citizens' Advice Bureaux and various other debt advice agencies, many people are wrongly encouraged to consolidate their debts into a single loan, which leaves them with no flexibility to prioritise repayments.

Others go to debt-management companies, which charge a fee for managing repayments and for distributing the money to creditors. This fee often equates to the first monthly payments, which means arrears continue to spiral.

Many debt-management companies fail to explain clearly that the first priorities are the mortgage or rent, council tax, utility bills, television licence and loans secured on a property. Failure to service these debts can lead to homelessness, imprisonment or withdrawal of utility supplies.

Other loans and credit or store card payments can often be rescheduled and non-payment results only in a poor credit record, difficulty in obtaining future credit and, at worst, bankruptcy or a County Court order to repay at a level the debtor can afford.

Failure to repay hire purchase debts can led to the car or household item being repossessed.

■ The National Debt Line can be contacted on 0808 808 4000

© Telegraph Group Limited, London 2003

£1bn power of the tweenagers

Pocket money up by 66 per cent. They prefer designer labels. And even pick family car

By Sean Poulter, Consumer Affairs Correspondent

At first glance, they may not seem like big spenders.

But retailers would be wise not to underestimate the power of the preteens – who have a combined income of £1 billion a year.

A study has found that the so-called 'tweenager' generation of children aged between ten and 13 has enjoyed a 66 per cent pay rise in just five years.

And they are not only choosing things for themselves.

The survey by retail analysts Datamonitor found that many children also have a say in family diet and even the choice of a new car or home.

In 1997, the spending power of UK tweenagers was £600 million, earned through pocket money, hand-outs and money for household chores.

Last year, that figure had soared to £1 billion as tweenagers cashed in on the guilt of absent parents.

According to today's report, many parents are prepared to indulge their children to make up for being away from home so often.

It said the breakdown of the traditional two-parent family, divorce and longer working hours are all contributing to this.

There are also fewer children aged ten to 13 in Britain – down 80,000 in five years to 2.79 million.

The average tweenager received £7.02 a week last year, including pocket money and extras. This was up dramatically from £4.02 a week in 1997.

Most of the money is spent on confectionery, snacks, soft drinks, magazines, music, make-up and personal care products.

But more and more is being spent on designer label clothes, sports gear and the latest mobile phones.

Piers Berezai, consumer analyst at Datamonitor, said: 'Parents are becoming more liberal and tolerant in their shopping patterns and many are allowing their children to decide which goods are bought for both them and the family.

'All this means that tweens not only have more money, they also have more autonomy over how it is spent and their influence on their parents' purchases is growing.'

But Mr Berezai suggested they may not always have it so good.

'Many parents are tightening their belts in the current economic environment and their concerns about the amount of advertising and marketing to children and the effects of over-indulging youths are growing,' he said.

'The result of these factors is that the rate of increase in tween pocket money, and other handouts, is slowing.'

In fact, the report forecasts that by 2007 the average income of a tweenager will have risen by a measly 5p a year to £7.27.

Datamonitor says fashion trends among tweens are short-lived as children between ten and 13 go through rapid personal development as they leave behind their childhood and enter their teenage years.

Mr Berezai said tweens often aspire to being around five years older than they actually are, with many 12-year-olds believing 17 is the ideal age.

Many also have adult tastes and their desire to age means they are often seeking, not just teen-based products, but also adult-orientated ones.

The report concludes that makers of food, drinks and personal care products would be better off not targeting tweenagers directly, but broadening the appeal of adult and teen-orientated brands to include the tweenager.

© *The Daily Mail* *January, 2003*

Study shows debt as a recipe for family friction

New research reveals conflict in families between saving and debt – and highlights problem of Britain's debt culture

Money in the Contemporary Family, a study for Nestlé Family Monitor, reveals a conflict in British families between the traditional savings ethic, and the apparent inevitability of debt in today's society. Children are becoming active consumers at an ever-younger age, students face rising debts, and concern grows that financial companies are too willing to lend money.

Project consultant Professor Alan Lewis, professor of economic psychology at the University of Bath, said: 'This unique study provides an important insight into attitudes toward money and debt. A fundamental conflict emerges between the traditional savings ethic, which remains strong in British families, and a belief that debt is unavoidable for many. There is evidence that this conflict is reinforced by government policies such as the Student Loan Scheme, and by the perceived willingness of financial institutions to lend money. There is real concern that we are creating a debt culture, which is effectively teaching young people that debt is normal and indeed inevitable for some people.'

Neither a borrower, nor a lender be. Is debt inevitable?

Changing attitudes towards savings and debt are revealed by the study.

Although the savings ethic remains strong – with 71% cent of respondents 'saving for a rainy day' – people believe that their parents were more prudent

---

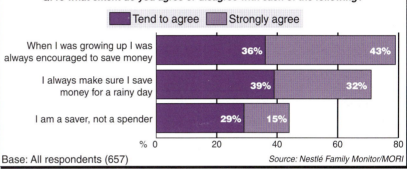

Saving money

Saving is viewed in a positive light and nearly four out of five respondents (79%) say they were encouraged to save money when they were growing up. This 'saving ethic' was most prevalent among respondents whose parents taught them a 'great deal' or a 'fair amount' about finances (90%) and those with a degree or higher (85%). Despite recent increases in credit use and debt this saving ethic has been impressed on the young with 84% of those aged 16-34 years claiming they were encouraged to save whilst young.

Q. To what extent do you agree or disagree with each of the following?

Legend: ■ Tend to agree   ■ Strongly agree

	Tend to agree	Strongly agree
When I was growing up I was always encouraged to save money	36%	43%
I always make sure I save money for a rainy day	39%	32%
I am a saver, not a spender	29%	15%

Base: All respondents (657)

Source: Nestlé Family Monitor/MORI

Although the savings ethic remains strong – with 71% cent of respondents 'saving for a rainy day' – people believe that their parents were more prudent. Fifty-nine per cent of respondents agree that it is inevitable you will get into debt nowadays. The perceived inevitability of debt is more pronounced among men (64%), 16-34-year-olds (76%), and respondents in Scotland and Wales (69% and 68% respectively).

Student loans and debt culture

At a time when one in three young people are entering higher education, the Student Loan Scheme provokes a mixed response. Overall, 47% of respondents favour the scheme, while 37% oppose it. However, the position is very different with respondents who have children in higher education with 73% believing that student loans encourage young people to become accustomed to borrowing, with negative consequences.

Fifty-five per cent of these respondents with children in higher education also agree that the Student Loan Scheme causes friction between students and their parents.

Who is responsible?

There is a strong feeling that financial companies are too willing to lend money – with as many as 90% agreeing with this view. Seventy-one per cent believe that the Government should do more to help people avoid debt.

Commenting on these findings, Professor Lewis said: 'People want to be prudent and save, yet debt is seen as inevitable among certain groups of society. While the government encourages savings through tax-free ISAs, it is as though they are legitimising debt through the Student Loan Scheme. People are prepared to take some responsibility for getting into financial difficulties but there are strong feelings that financial companies should lend more responsibly and the government should provide more protection for consumers.'

Too much, too young. Teaching children about money

As children become active consumers at an ever-younger age, parents are teaching their children more about financial matters, but want schools to participate in this activity, the study shows. Sixty-two per cent of parents have given their children piggy banks and 46% have set up bank accounts for their children. However, 59% of parents thought schools taught just a little or nothing at all about money matters. In particular, parents would like schools to teach children about careers, personal finance, and understanding the use of credit and debit cards.

Professor Lewis said: 'There is a strong desire for schools to provide teaching in personal finance – a result which should strengthen the resolve of the Financial Services Agency and the Department for Education and Employment in the preparation of curriculum resources on personal finance. The results also support calls by the Personal Finance Education Group to include personal finance

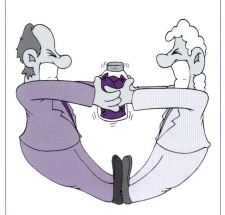

education in the national curriculum.'

Who wears the trousers?

Within the home, financial decision-making is becoming more democratic. Men no longer make most of the larger financial decisions, the study shows. Fifty-nine per cent of married couples share a joint bank account and both contribute to

financial decisions. Only 32% of unmarried couples living together organise their finances in this way.

Who wants to be a millionaire?

The survey also reveals that while everyone may want to be a millionaire, 61% of respondents would settle for £64,000 or less to change the quality of their lives.

■ For the Nestlé Family Monitor study on *Money in the Contemporary Family*, 657 adults, aged 16 plus (of which 81 had children at university), were interviewed face to face in home by MORI in 60 sampling points across Great Britain between 7 April and 23 April 2001. The Nestlé Family Monitor is part of a series of research studies into family life in Britain undertaken on behalf of Nestlé by MORI.

© 2002 MORI

You're never too young to spend, spend, spend

Pocket money and earnings give children real buying power. Jill Papworth discovers where their money comes from . . . and what they like to spend it on

Where do children get their money from?

In the UK they receive an average of £5.79 a week, according to the Halifax's latest Pocket Money Survey of seven to 16-year-olds. Boys outstrip girls with an average £6.18 a week against £5.38 for girls.

£2 is the most common weekly amount in the seven to 10 age group, received by one in four, while one in five gets £5. Among 11 to 16-year-olds, one in three receives £5, while one in five gets £10.

Some 86% receive regular pocket money from their parents and 16% get it from their grandparents, though this rises to 30% amongst seven-year-olds.

Research from financial services provider Goldfish finds three quarters of seven to 16-year-olds receive an average £6.70 a week. Some 65% of

15 to 16-year-olds get a regular 'allowance' from parents. Of those, almost one in four gets more than £60 a month and almost one in 10 more than £100.

Many children take on part-time jobs. The Halifax found that nearly one in four 11 to 16-year-olds have a part-time job earning, on average, £27.31 a week. That rises to

---

British children are neglecting to save. Only 19% put money in a bank or building society and of 15 to 16-year-olds, just 24% have a savings account

---

58% of 16-year-olds on £42.20. The most popular job is a paper round (24%), followed by working in a shop (17%) and in pubs and restaurants (13%). Some 3% of seven to 10-year-olds claim to have a job.

What do they do with it?

The third most popular home for their cash, is a bank or building society savings account, says the Halifax. Children in the seven to 10 age group are more likely to save all, or most, of their money (26%) than 11 to 16-year-olds (11%). Children in the north are most likely to bank their money (38%), while those in the midlands (27%) are the least likely.

Research by Goldfish last year suggested British children are neglecting to save. It found that only 19% put money in a bank or building society and of 15- to 16-year-olds, just 24% have a savings account. Goldfish's marketing director Charlie Herbert said: 'What is worrying, but not surprising, is how little children save.'

A Mintel report into children's spending habits shows saving becomes considerably harder with age. By the time children reach the ages of 11 to 16, some 46% say they are no good at saving. The same number say that they spend money without thinking.

The spend, spend, spend philosophy seems more attractive to girls than boys, says the Halifax report, with only 20% of girls saying they save more than they spend compared to 28% of boys.

Spending patterns for seven- to 10-year-olds have changed, compared to previous Halifax surveys. Popular purchases are still sweets, magazines and toys, but computer games, holidays and CDs are favourites with this age group. For 11- to 16-year-olds, the most popular things to spend on include clothes, going out, CDs/tapes, mobile phones and computer games with books bottom of the list.

When putting cash away is a family affair

Local government officer Tracey Lewis and her husband Ian, a motor technician, have set their sights far ahead. They are saving for university fees for Helin, nearly three, and brother Dyfan, 11 months. 'I started putting £60 a month child benefit for Helin into a Britannic policy when she was born. It is intended for when she is 18 – she should have £15,000 or more,' says Tracey, 34. 'Then the Britannic rep lost his job and became an independent financial adviser. He told us about Children's Mutual – the old Tunbridge Wells.'

Tracey and Ian, who live in Carmarthenshire, liked its tax-free plans and the security that they have to repay at least the amount they put in. 'We signed up for each of us and for Dyfan at £20 a month. Having it in three parts means the whole £60 a month is in a tax-free fund – otherwise it would just be £25 into the plan,' she says.

The spend, spend, spend philosophy seems more attractive to girls than boys with only 20% of girls saying they save more than they spend compared to 28% of boys

---

'These policies are their only savings – and we do not have anything more than some cash in the bank. This is a family investment.'

New parents should feel the benefit

Parents can help themselves to help their children by ensuring they don't miss out on what's theirs. So we asked kids and money expert David White, Chief Executive of the Children's Mutual, what he would do.

- Check out with your local tax office to see if you're entitled to the new Children's Tax Credit or Working Families' Tax Credit that comes into force in April. Parents with a joint income below £54,000 can apply – £66,000 if you have a new-born child.

- New parents should think about saving Child Benefit for their offspring before they get used to spending it. Child Benefit increases to £16.05 per week from April for the first child – almost £70 a month. Or save half after using £35 to help with the nappy bills.

- Save regularly and early – it is much more expensive to leave it.

- Be organised: claim back tax on bank and building society savings accounts. And if one partner is not working, transfer savings to the non-taxpayer.

- Be disciplined: cut down on non-essential items such as the occasional pint, magazine or chocolate bar. By giving up just 2 1/2 pints of beer a week, you could save around £25 a month.

- Live within your means: don't enter into financial agreements such as credit cards, loans, store cards or hire purchase agreements unless you need them (not want them) and you are sure you can repay.

- Know what you have – audit your own finances so your money really works for you – not the bank or credit card company.

© *Guardian Newspapers Limited 2003*

Spending money			
Children's average weekly spending looks like this (£)			
	All children	**Boys**	**Girls**
Clothes	2.53	1.92	3.17
Going out	2.44	2.17	2.73
Savings	2.41	2.74	2.05
CDs/tapes	1.96	1.85	2.07
Mobile phone	1.80	1.76	1.85
Gifts	1.66	1.46	1.86
Computer games	1.62	2.63	0.52
Sweets	1.31	1.42	1.18
Sportswear	1.26	1.62	0.86
Holidays	1.02	0.96	1.07
Magazines	1.01	1.01	1.01
Videos	0.94	0.96	0.91
Cosmetics	0.91	0.35	1.52
Food	0.87	1.12	0.61
Drinnks	0.84	0.93	0.75
Bus/train fares	0.65	0.67	0.62
Books	0.57	0.56	0.59

Source: Halifax Pocket Money Survey 2003

Cash in hand

Money's too tight to mention? Not according to the teenagers who recently told Anita Pati how they earn and spend their cash

How important is money to teenagers – and how do they manage on what they get? A recent survey suggests many young people have a sophisticated approach to finance, and are also very concerned about financial security in the future. The study *Young Lives, Our Future* was published in June 2003 by children's charity NCH and Norwich Union and was based on interviews with 13- to 19-year-olds. A key finding was that teenagers' top worries for the future were 'not getting a job' (35 per cent) and 'getting into debt' (17 per cent). Almost nine in 10 have a bank or building society account with three-quarters of teenagers having savings. Parents and family are very important sources of information about money and three-quarters depend on them for advice.

Teenagers out and about in London told *0-19* about their money and how they manage it, and their answers backed up this research. Billie, 13, and Gemma, 14, described their earning and spending patterns. Billie posts leaflets for three hours on Monday and Tuesday evenings for her aunt. For this she gets a total of £10. She also works every Saturday for £15 then gets £5 from each parent at weekends, who also save £2 per week for her.

Gemma gets £10 each from her mother and father each weekend. They also save £2 a week for her in an insurance policy which will yield £2,000 when she turns 16. Her own bank balance stands at £800. She thinks it is good to save but has no idea what she'll do with the money. She doesn't have a job at the moment but is looking: 'You can't get jobs,' she says, 'but hairdressers will sometimes take you on. That's what I want to do.'

A recent survey suggests many young people have a sophisticated approach to finance, and are also very concerned about financial security in the future

---

They get together with friends in the high street usually but occasionally go swimming at the local lido or to the fast-food chain Nando's. Some of their money goes in directions their parents might not approve of if they knew about it. 'I spend it on alcohol, cigarettes and puff,' she says, giggling. She and her other friends get older children 'or ask adults in the street' to buy it for them. Vodka and Lambrini are favourites. They tend to drink in the park or in friends' gardens when parents are away. Gemma doesn't drink or smoke as much as she used to – 'only on the odd occasion now'.

Both girls are happy with the amount of money they get and it doesn't cause rows within the family. 'The only thing I get into trouble for is getting in late,' says Billie.

The odd pound here and there is often saved rather than squandered. Grant, 17, and his sister Becky, 14, were visiting London from the North West to visit relatives. Although their parents finance their routine spending, both siblings make a habit of putting away money whenever they can. Becky babysits every Friday for her younger brother for £2 then every few months she will get around £10 for looking after a family friend's children. She gets £4 a week pocket money from her parents. 'Mainly my parents buy my clothes so I spend it on books quite a lot.' She doesn't get whatever she wants, just 'serious stuff', but is happy with what she has.

She also has a savings account. 'It's good because I get interest. I save out of my pocket money and if

---

Money – earning it

We asked teenagers how they earned their money. These days, teenagers are juggling school with a working life. Half of teens (69% of 17- to 19-year-olds and 35% of 13- to 16-year-olds) get most of their money from their jobs. The number of teens who get most of their money from a job is highest in the Midlands – 55%. Those who receive most of their money from parents are given it regularly as pocket money rather than on demand.

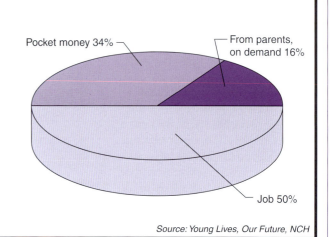

Pocket money 34%

From parents, on demand 16%

Job 50%

Source: Young Lives, Our Future, NCH

I've got anything left after I've shopped or whatever, or when I've been babysitting.' She puts away about £5 per month.

Grant, 17, has just finished his AS-levels. He works four hours every Saturday in a pet-food factory which earns him £10 per week. This is his pocket money. His parents buy clothes and toiletries for him. 'My parents will buy me stuff I really need like clothes but I have to save up to buy other stuff like computer upgrades, DVDs and CDs.

'I save up for the biggest stuff – I just went to America and that cost quite a bit.'

He is comfortable with what he has 'although I always want more', and doesn't think his Saturday job affects his college work. A friend of his was not so lucky though: 'He used to do a lot of work which did affect his school work. He was doing a paper round so he had to be there in the mornings before college, seven days a week. He got quite a bit for it – £25 per week. But he had to give it up in the end.'

Anji, 17, is at sixth form college doing her A-levels. She has never worked and gets money from her parents whenever she needs

something. 'I probably get about £40 per month. When I'm going shopping on my own I have to pay for my own stuff with the money they give me but if I'm going with my mum, she pays. The £40 is for CDs, clothes, concert tickets and stuff.'

Anji is more confident than the others about her income. She does have a bank account but doesn't use it. 'I'm thinking of a summer job but I haven't done anything about it yet. I would like to work in a shop kind of thing, a CD or maybe a clothes shop because you'd get discounts. I wouldn't fancy waitressing.

'My little sister, who's 12, gets money too but I don't think she needs it as much as older people like me. She doesn't go out with friends as much as I do. At her age, they go round to friends' houses. It affects

people my age more. Some of my friends say: "I can't go out this weekend because I haven't got enough money."'

Dan, 18, has just finished his A-levels and is financially dependent on his mother, a lone parent. 'I'm looking for a job before I go to university. I get all my money from my mum but I need to save up over the summer so that I don't get into massive debt at university. I don't get a set amount per week, just when I need it.'

He has his own bank account 'but that's just savings. I don't have an income so I put in money from what I get on birthdays or Christmas, or from my grandparents.'

Most teenagers I spoke to feel some responsibility for their own money management, even if their visions were slightly vague. 'I don't know what I'm saving for really,' says Becky. 'I'm just saving in case it's useful one day. You see all these people getting into debt and you think "I don't want to be one of them".'

■ The above information is from *0-19 Magazine's* web site which can be found at www.zero2nineteen.co.uk

© 0-19 Magazine

Is a cashless society on the cards?

Debit and credit cards are everywhere, helping us to buy our groceries, our luxuries and our dreams without the need to resort to coins and cash.

There are two billion credit cards on high streets across the globe: they're part of our culture.

Britain is now spending more on plastic than cash and cheques and there are more than 60 different issuers, from banks and building societies to football clubs, offering a bewildering array of 1,500 different cards.

It seems the experts are at last being proved right. At the dawn of the technologically advanced 21st century we are turning into a cashless society, where the purse and the

wallet are being made redundant as we instead slip a couple of cards into our pocket as we head out the front door.

A decade ago this would have been unthinkable. Shopping trips required you to go out with plenty of notes and your cheque book in tow. Cards were reserved for large

---

Britain is now spending more on plastic than cash and cheques and there are more than 60 different issuers

---

purchases, but cash was still king when it came to everyday items.

But plastic has edged into our national lifestyle and most shoppers now use credit cards without batting an eyelid. Research from More Than shows that a fifth of all credit card transactions are for less than £10. One in four is for less than £20.

It's not just on the high street that cash is losing its lustre, however. Millions of people now pay their household bills by direct debit, buy electronically on the internet and have their wages and benefits paid straight into their bank accounts.

The days when workers would queue to receive their weekly pay packet in notes and coins have long gone.

But is the cashless society fact or fiction? Is it possible to only pay for your 35p copy of *The Journal* or £1.85 mid-morning cup of coffee with your 'flexible friend'? Would you be laughed out of the corner store if you wanted to put your 15p apple 'on the plastic'?

To find out, I decided to see if I could spend an average day in Newcastle with nothing but my debit card to fall back on.

And to make the experiment fair, three volunteers agreed to help.

Vicky Hutchinson, 33, is a cattery worker from Slaley, in the heart of rural Northumberland, while Nickie Gott, 37, is a married mother of two who runs her own events business, She's Gott It, from her semi-urban home near Chester-le-Street, County Durham.

Last week we set ourselves the task of trying to buy such mundane items as a morning newspaper, cup of coffee, lunch, and after-work drink without the aid of cash. This is what happened.

Vicky Hutchinson

I start work at 8am, so there was nowhere open in Slaley for me to go and buy a newspaper at that hour of the day.

I popped into the post office in the village later on, but it doesn't take cards of any kind. It sells groceries as well as doing all the normal things a post office does but the owner said she had never been asked to accept a card before. There isn't really any need – most people only buy one or two items and the older people tend to use their pension money which they pick up from the post office anyway.

Mid-morning I drove into Hexham and had a coffee at a small café, but I couldn't use my debit card there either. I was told it is because the bank charges for each transaction. The owner said she has had to let people dash out to the cashpoint.

Lunch-time I went to a bakery shop in Hexham and bought some buns and a sticky doughnut, but I had to use cash. Neither would any of the butchers' or grocers' shops in the middle of the town take cards.

Buying petrol on my debit card

wasn't a problem but I couldn't get a drink at my local pub. You certainly can't survive without cash around this area. I knew before I started this experiment that I was going to have trouble. At the moment it doesn't worry me as I get paid in cash and very rarely have to withdraw money from the bank or a cashpoint machine but if I started being paid directly into my bank account I would be stuck. I would have to go to Hexham or Consett to use a cashpoint machine or get cashback from one of the big supermarkets. That would involve both time and money in petrol costs.

Public transport wouldn't be an option; it is limited and you can't buy a ticket without cash. Having worked for my father who had his own business, I know it costs to operate electronic card payment machines, so if you accept small payments, say from £1 to £10, your profit margin is dramatically reduced.

It would make it easier if I didn't have to bother about cash. I would only have to carry one thing instead of a purse full of notes and coins.

'Unless things change dramatically, I can't see a time where we will ever be a cashless society'

But I am of the old school; I like to be able to pay for things. I do have a credit card but I don't use it that often. I'm terrible at remembering to pay the bill. I prefer to pay for things straight out and have it done and dusted.

Unless things change dramatically, I can't see a time where we will ever be a cashless society. It would be impossible to survive in an area like Slaley. Cards have their place but they are no use to me on a day-to-day basis.

Nickie Gott

I organise events and do the marketing and public relations for them. I operate from home in Great Lumley, Chester-le-Street, County Durham, and an average day will see me out and about meeting clients as well as taking my children, Francesca, 12, and Harrison, 10, to after-school activities.

I have to admit I'm useless at carrying cash. I'll be out with the children and forever rummaging in the bottom of my bag for some money. The reason is I usually tend to go to places where I can use my card.

I buy my groceries at the local Co-op and if I need it, I can get cashback too. If I need extra money, I'm just around the corner from a cashpoint machine.

Most of my life is card-orientated. I don't know at the start of the week how much cash I am going to need to get me through to Friday. I'm not that organised. Some weeks I may only spend £20 cash and others it may be hundreds.

This particular day I started off at home, had a mid-morning meeting just up the road, then popped into Newcastle before ending up in Durham City in the afternoon. My first stop was my local newsagent. It doesn't take cards of any kind so I wasn't able to get a paper. I drove to my meeting at Durham's Riverside cricket ground. There's a very nice bar and bistro there which I use a lot. I got coffees and was able to use my Switch card. Usually you have to spend a minimum of £5 if you want to use your card, but they put it through at just over £4. I drove to Newcastle and ended up having a late lunch in Durham City. I bought a sandwich, a small bag of grapes and a drink at Marks & Spencer for just over £4. I was asked if I wanted any cashback and I had no problem using my Switch.

I go to my local garage for fuel. I have a business card and had no problem using it. I can't think there would be many garages that don't take cards, especially when you consider what a full tank of petrol costs. Having said that, I do know of one garage in the Durham area where you have to spend more than £10 before they will accept a card.

I needed a few groceries so popped into Chester-le-Street. I would normally go to the Co-op, but thought I would try the smaller shops. None would take a card, so I ended up at the Co-op anyway.

I suffer from hayfever and needed some tablets, so I popped into my local pharmacy. I was impressed as not only did they volunteer to take my payment by card, but offered cashback as well.

But is the cashless society fact or fiction? Is it possible to only pay for your 35p copy of The Journal or £1.85 mid-morning cup of coffee with your 'flexible friend?'

That night I went to a pub near home for an after-work drink. I asked if I could use my card and was told I would have to spend at least £5. So I couldn't buy a £1 drink on my Switch, but I would have been able to if I had taken up the offer of cash back, which would have taken the bill to more than £5.

The other alternative would have been to keep an open tab going all night and pay at the end of the evening, but I didn't like the idea of leaving my card behind the bar.

As I usually only go to places where I can use my card, I have been surprised how many stores still won't accept them or require a minimum spend. Some shops that wouldn't take my card wouldn't accept a cheque for less than £5 either.

The comment I got from the newsagent was that it costs them for every transaction, so I suppose I can understand that smaller businesses don't want to take cards. Bigger companies probably absorb the cost or pass it on to the customer in prices.

This experiment has made me realise we are a long way from being a cashless society. It isn't a problem for me because I know where I can use my card and gravitate to those places. But I could find it awkward if I were to end up somewhere un-familiar with no cash.

Jane Hall

'My journey into the realms of the cashless society ground to a halt before I had even started my day. I travel to work by Metro but the ticket machines only take coins. Luckily I have an annual travel pass.

I didn't fair much better when I tried to buy *The Journal* at various newsagents in the city centre. No cash, no deal was the answer when I asked whether my debit card would be accepted for the 35p.

Next was my takeaway coffee. The first place I tried didn't accept cards. Surprisingly, I couldn't get a coffee at Starbucks either. The chain accepts credit cards, but not debit. There is no minimum payment, however, so with the right card it would have been possible for me to buy a £1.75 coffee.

Buying lunch was little better. None of the sandwich bars within

easy walking distance of *The Journal*'s offices would take my debit card. Luckily there is a Boots on the corner of Grainger and Newgate streets and I was able to buy a pre-packed sandwich, packet of crisps, yoghurt and a bottle of still water with my card.

The bill came to £3.60 but I was told there is no minimum spend. Even better, I earned 14 Boots Advantage card points.

Attempts to buy fresh fruit and vegetables at Newcastle's large indoor market on my debit card were met with scornful shakes of the head by the stallholders, so instead I headed for Safeway where staff were only too pleased to take my money in whatever form it came – and offer me cashback.

Of the four pubs and bars I tried in the city centre, all had a minimum £5 spend for card users.

There was a pleasant surprise at the end of the day, though. Having forgotten I had no cash on me, an art shop in Monument Mall volunteered to take my debit card in payment for a £1.65 birthday card. When I suggested it was too small an amount to bother with, the assistant said: 'It's no trouble. We'd much prefer it if you shopped with us than not.'

Perhaps that's the problem – rather than the customer calling the shots, it is business which now dictates how and when we spend. Many believe they are doing us a favour by taking our money.

Working in Newcastle, I had expected it to be relatively easy to get through the day without cash. But I seemed to be thwarted at every turn. I like the freedom to be able to choose how I pay and not to have to worry if I have enough money in my purse.

© Owned by or licensed to
Trinity Mirror Plc 2003

The moneywise generation

By Jo Thornhill,
Mail on Sunday

Teaching children how to handle money is likely to spread to more schools, thanks to the vision of a new charity chief.

Lessons in personal finance have been part of the national curriculum for more than three years, aided by the Personal Finance Education Group, a charity that brings the finance industry and schools together and provides resources for teachers.

The group was given a further boost last week with the appointment as chairman of Ron Sandler, who carried out a high-profile review of the retail savings industry for the Government last year. He has great hopes for the charity's role in the education system.

Sandler says: 'The review I carried out highlighted the need for more financially literate and empowered consumers. I believe we can start to tackle that.

'The group has already made a great start in helping teachers. Our challenge now is to make sure our resources are used in as many schools as possible.'

Among the initiatives is an 'excellence and access' scheme, which began in September 2001. The project links specialist advisers with teachers to train them in personal finance and help with lesson planning.

The scheme has reached only 400 secondary schools in England, but Sandler wants to broaden it to as many as possible, including those in Scotland, Northern Ireland and Wales.

Deborah Shields at National Debtline, the free debt-advice helpline based in Birmingham, believes teaching about money matters, particularly debt, is vital. She says borrowing, excluding mortgage debt, has never been higher. The figure has now topped £150 billion, according to the Bank of England.

She adds: 'The earlier people learn about managing money the better. No one can anticipate changes in life, such as divorce or redundancy, but if they are equipped to deal with these problems and understand how interest rates work and how to shop around for a good deal, that is definitely going to help.'

Catford Girls' School in south London has been part of the excellence and access scheme since last September. The group's advisers have been liaising with staff to help with lessons covering issues such as borrowing and credit, overdrafts and household bills, ethical investments and Muslim mortgages.

Ruth Holden, the school's assistant head teacher, believes personal finance education has an important part to play in schools and that the more practical and enjoyable the lessons, the more students will want to learn.

She says: 'It's important, particularly for girls, to understand how to handle money and deal with finances.

'The support that the group has offered has been excellent for our teachers and since we know the resources we're using have their approval, we can be confident that we are teaching to a high standard and our students will benefit.'

© 2003 Associated Newspapers Ltd

> *'It's important, particularly for girls, to understand how to handle money and deal with finances'*

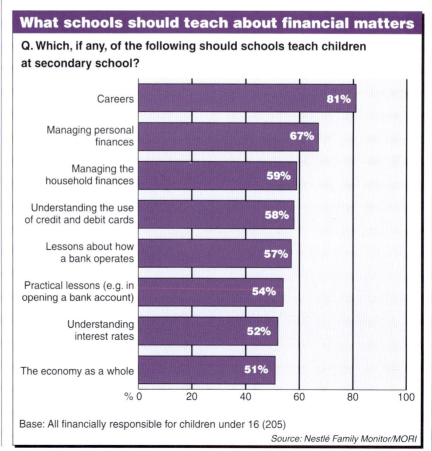

What schools should teach about financial matters

Q. Which, if any, of the following should schools teach children at secondary school?

	%
Careers	81%
Managing personal finances	67%
Managing the household finances	59%
Understanding the use of credit and debit cards	58%
Lessons about how a bank operates	57%
Practical lessons (e.g. in opening a bank account)	54%
Understanding interest rates	52%
The economy as a whole	51%

Base: All financially responsible for children under 16 (205)

Source: Nestlé Family Monitor/MORI

Vital lessons

By Clare Hall, *Mail on Sunday*

First they want football strips and micro scooters, which leave little change from £60. Then they want Nike trainers for £80 and mini-disc Walkmans for £120 and PlayStations for £200.

It makes you wonder. Do our children have any idea of the value of money? The fact that they are growing up in an almost cashless society does not help.

From a young age, most children see their parents paying with plastic – in the supermarket, in restaurants, in shops, on holiday. In fact, research shows that children from the poorest families are often more financially literate than those from affluent families simply because their parents are more likely to use cash.

Parents are also less likely than past generations to give their children pocket money. Instead, sweets, toys and books are often picked up at the supermarket during the weekly shopping trips.

As a result, young children are growing up with poor financial skills and this could lead to serious problems in adulthood.

The Personal Finance Education Group (PFEG), a London-based charity, was set up four years ago to try to tackle the problem. As financial support from the state continues to dwindle, the PFEG believes it is vital for young people to learn about solvency and saving.

Last year, it introduced Excellence and Access – a four-year education programme that aims to teach pupils money-management skills.

Subjects covered include budgeting, understanding credit and debt, ethical investment and learning to be financially independent.

So far, however, the PFEG has focused its efforts on children in secondary schools and it falls to parents to teach their younger offspring about money. But where do parents start?

Ann-Marie Blake who runs Face2Face With Finance, NatWest bank's financial education programme for schools, believes parents should teach by example. She says: 'It's all about involving your children in day-to-day money management. From a very early age you can introduce them to coins and teach them to recognise the different values.'

It is also a good idea to find out exactly how much, or little, your child understands about money.

To help with this, we have joined forces with the Children's Mutual Friendly Society which has produced a book of money-related board games called Making Sense Of Money. (Available free of charge on 0800 585474.)

There are other ways to introduce money at home. From the age of two or three, most young children will enjoy playing shops with a till full of real money and groceries labelled with prices.

You could have sales at the shop, offering two items for a pound and so on. Children who are learning to count will enjoy listening and counting while you drop some coins into a tin.

When you are doing the weekly shopping, ask older children to see how much each item costs and what the final total is at the checkout. And when Christmas comes round again, ask some friends and relatives to consider giving your child cash.

You never know – it might just be the encouragement they need to start saving.

Bank on an early start to savings

The best way to encourage a child's interest in money is to open a savings account for them. This is money management at its simplest.

From six or seven, your child can take cash or cheques to the building society or bank, hand it to the cashier and have the satisfaction of seeing the money grow.

The good news is that this is the one area where banks and building societies are relatively generous. It is not uncommon to find interest rates on children's accounts reaching almost 5%, far more than most adults manage to earn on their savings.

The reason for this is twofold. Banks and building societies want to reach new customers as young as possible. They can also afford to pay higher interest on the small amounts that children save. It makes sense to bank pocket money and cash gifts in an instant access account so children can save for something special.

Look out for Bradford & Bingley's Kidzone account, which pays 4.7% on balances of £1, Britannia building society's First Saver account, which pays 4.7% on balances of £1, and Halifax's Monthly Saver, which pays 5% on balances of £5 or more.

Away from the high street, Saffron Walden building society's Ladybird account pays 4.7% on minimum deposits of £1, and Loughborough building society pays 4.6% to Penguin account holders on balances of £10 or more.

Children's bonds offer a good way of encouraging long-term saving. The money is locked in at a fixed rate for a set term – say three or four years – after which it can either be spent, reinvested in another bond or put into a savings account. Children receive annual statements showing how much interest their bond has earned. Look at Cheshire building society's four-year Black Cat Bond, which pays 4.88% on minimum deposits of £500, Dunfermline building society's three-year Children's Bond, which pays 4.5% on minimum deposits of £100 and Abbey National's four-year Savings Bond, which pays 4.4% on a minimum of £500.

■ Editor's Note: The above interest rates may have changed since the publication of this article.

© 2003 Associated Newspapers Ltd

You and your money

Managing money successfully is an essential skill no matter how much you earn. It is also one of the hardest things to do in life. It's easy to spend money, but just as easy to overspend and land yourself in trouble. Without a proper plan and attitude, we run the risk of wrecking our hopes, our relationships and our health

Learning the basics

We're so used to money from an early age that we often treat it carelessly. But if we followed a few basic rules and gradually developed an understanding of how to look after it and make it work for us, we'd all be better off – in more ways than one.

The first money we lay our hands on in life is usually pocket money. Normally, we can spend it as we please: on clothes, CDs, snacks, entertainment. But when we leave home, we can't be so free with it. That's when money has a number of vital roles to play in life, providing such essentials as:

- a roof over our head
- food on our plate
- heat and light
- everyday items for the home
- travel expenses
- a TV licence
- council tax.

It's also important for our well-being to have some leisure time and that too must be paid for. Equally, we must think of the future and make money work for us. Without a plan of action, we are very soon going to find that we're struggling.

Make a budget

If you're about to leave home or you have just left home, it's a smart move to draw up a plan or budget showing:

- what you need to survive – to include leisure expenses and essentials
- how much money you receive by way of a job or/and benefits.

It's a good idea to overestimate what you need to survive. There are always life's little surprises to provide for like buying a suit for a special occasion.

In the end, you may find that your needs are greater than the money you receive. Don't panic! Another look at all those needs may help you find where you can make cuts. For example, do you need to go out five times a week? Would it be better to eat out less often? When

you do go out, set yourself a spending limit and stick to it.

Finding an evening or weekend job can help make up the difference or just give you extra cash, especially if you're a student or a low-paid worker. Don't forget, when you're working in a restaurant or a bar, you're not spending. And a part-time job is a good way of meeting new people and having new experiences. It can also look good on your CV.

Once you've set the balance right between what you need to survive and what you earn, you may find you have a surplus. This can be set aside for an annual holiday or for a car or bike. Be strict with yourself. Work out a realistic time when you can have that holiday or buy that bike. Too soon, and you'll be putting too much aside and running yourself short on other things.

Day-to-day budgeting

Once you've drawn up a list of essentials you need to survive, that's

not the end of it. In order to make sure you can balance things out by the end of a week or a month, you have to keep an eye on spending.

For instance, if your favourite daily sandwich goes up 25p, think about switching to a less expensive sandwich. Or look out for a cheaper sandwich bar. It's a small sacrifice and think what you'll be saving. Yes, it's only 25p. But that's over £1 a week. And if you can economise on one small, insignificant item in your daily routine, think how you might be able to save on all the other items on your list. By the end of a month you might actually be making an unexpected profit. Of course you could start making your own sandwich every morning and then you'd really be saving money!

Beware of credit

It's so easy to get what you want nowadays. Once you're 18 – the age when you're allowed to borrow money – everyone seems to be bending over backwards to lend you money or offer you credit. But don't let it go to your head. They're not doing this because they like you. They're doing it because they want to make money out of you. Watch those interest rates. Some store cards, for example, charge more than regular credit cards.

And don't be tempted to buy an expensive DVD player, television or second-hand car just because it says 'You pay nothing for six months.' Ask yourself whether you're really going to be able to pay more easily in six months.

■ Are you going to get promotion in your job?
■ Are you finishing college? In which case are you anticipating getting a job you haven't got yet?
■ Are your outgoings (what you

Once you're 18 – the age when you're allowed to borrow money – everyone seems to be bending over backwards to lend you money or offer you credit

---

spend) going to be less? They might be more.

And look at the small print. You might find that after six months you're landed with higher interest rates than other credit agreements.

Two golden rules to remember:
■ whatever you buy, you're going to have to pay for it some time.
■ don't buy on impulse. If need be, go away and think about major purchases. Ask someone you know and trust what they think.

Putting some money aside

Living for the moment might seem like a good idea. But if you want to get the best out of life then you need to plan for tomorrow – and a whole load of other tomorrows.

Saving money is not such a bad idea. It can:
■ make your money work for you
■ provide a foundation for future purchases
■ help when borrowing more money in the future.

Some form of investment plan can be started to help you put money safely away. Talk to one of the local high street banks or building societies. They'll be happy to give you literature on a variety of schemes. But whatever plan you choose, you'd be well advised to discuss it with an independent financial adviser (IFA). Many people do because money matters can often seem like doing algebra in a foreign language.

On the other hand, don't buy or invest in anything you don't fully understand. It's your right to ask for a fuller explanation. If they're not prepared to spend their time explaining the detail, don't give them your money.

Future purchases could cover anything from a car to a 'once in a lifetime' opportunity to go travelling with friends. Money already saved could help pay for expenses and act as something to fall back on when you get home.

A savings account or savings plan could also help when borrowing money for major purchases like a house. If you can put up a lump sum you could get a better deal. Not only that, but with savings behind you lenders will be happier to advance you your loan.

If you can only set aside a few pounds a week, it's better than nothing. It'll also get you into the habit of saving. When you get that better job you can always 'up' the amount you put away.

Insurance

There are many forms of insurance but, in general, you need to be aware of two main types:
■ life insurance
■ general insurance.

Life insurance is a type of investment taken out for a period of time (or term) which pays out when someone dies. If they survive the term they receive a lump sum.

General insurance covers property and 'expensive to replace' possessions such as:
■ a house or a flat
■ cars, motorbikes or bikes
■ expensive games systems
■ mini disc players
■ computers.

Other than covering loss, general insurance can provide for the cost of repairing an item like a DVD player. However, general insurance cannot take into account sentimental value. If a bracelet is quite valuable it's up to you to get a valuation and tell the insurance company. If it gets lost, it's no good saying it's valuable because it belonged to your granny.

Insurers are risk takers. They will work out what the risk is when you insure something and so set the premium you'll have to pay. Suppose you want to insure the contents of your flat or house against burglary. If you're living in a high crime area your premium is going to be higher than if you were living in an area of low crime. Usually, insurers also see a young person with a car or motorbike as a high risk.

Debt

You can't borrow money or own a credit card until you're 18. But even if you haven't reached that age, it's important to know about the consequences of debt and how to get out of it.

Owing money to creditors is quite normal. For example, few people can buy a property outright. Instead, you borrow money from a reputable lender and pay it back over a period of time. Fewer still go shopping with a couple of suitcases stuffed full of money. This is the age of plastic so it's accepted that many people have a balance to pay off on a credit card. As long as repayments don't eat into other essentials such as food and electricity, they can be managed.

But because it's so simple to buy on credit, the repayments can get larger and larger. That's when it's easy to get into trouble.

If you have run up a series of debts and creditors are starting to send you threatening letters, keep calm. The first thing you must do is to put a halt on any spending other than necessities, like food. Take a long hard look at what has got you into debt. You might need to alter your lifestyle and cut back on everything but essentials.

Talking to creditors

Once in debt, the worst thing you can do is avoid your creditors. For one thing, they might think you're trying to dodge them. For another, they might think you're not taking your responsibilities seriously.

As soon as you realise things have got out of hand, make a financial plan. Start by drawing up a list of priorities such as:

- rent/mortgage
- weekly food bill for your house-hold
- gas, electricity
- fares/petrol to get to college/work
- cost of running your own car/ motorbike (to include road tax, insurance, etc.)
- cost of material for work – e.g. tools, books for a course, etc.

Tell your creditors how much you earn (together with any benefits) and how much you anticipate you'll be able to pay back over a period of

Saving money

Q. Have you put any of your own money into a savings scheme in the last 7 days?

More males than females are savers, with little difference between the year groups for those who save anything

Source: Young People in 2000, Schools Health Education Unit

time. Don't be tempted to reassure them with wild claims about your ability to pay them back. They'll be more impressed by regular small amounts than by promises of large amounts at irregular intervals.

Creditors appreciate honesty. Arrange to go and see them if possible. Follow everything up with a letter and keep a copy. It's your record of what you're doing to get yourself out of debt.

Getting out of debt

Offer to pay creditors the original amount rather than the interest. Sometimes they might be willing to settle for that if they can set a time limit on the repayment.

Take a long hard look at what has got you into debt. You might need to alter your lifestyle and cut back on everything but essentials

---

Try, if you can, not to borrow off friends. Debt can ruin relationships and no matter how good a friend someone is, when it comes to money, people often change. Also avoid borrowing off a loan 'shark'. These are people who will advance generous amounts of cash without asking for reference or security. The interest on the loans are usually very high and the terms can put you at a serious disadvantage. If you are in debt to that kind of lender, you can always go to court. The court may agree that your repayments are too high and order them to be cut.

But don't use the legal route as a way out of every debt situation. What you may think is high, the court may think is reasonable.

Think very carefully about taking on another loan to pay your way out. All you're probably doing is getting out of one hole by digging yourself another. If in doubt consult a professional financial adviser. You can get free advice from people in the know.

It might be possible to return some goods, assuming they've been recently purchased and are in good condition. If not, then they certainly have second-hand value. Selling them off may help some way towards getting you back in credit.

Making a will

It's never too early to make a will. On average, people have more possessions or assets than they think. By making a will, you say what you want done with your estate whether it be money or possessions.

- The above information is from Lifetime Careers Wiltshire Ltd. Visit their web site at www.lifetime-publishing.co.uk

© Lifetime Careers Wiltshire Ltd, 2003

Managing your own bank account

Managing the money in your bank account

Managing money is not an easy task, especially if you never have enough of it. But not managing money can be even worse, if you find yourself spending what you don't have. With the wide range of payment methods available and the temptations to spend on credit, it is easy to lose track of your finances by spending on things which are not a priority.

Here are some of the reasons people end up buying things that aren't a priority:

the assistant is friendly or helpful and so you feel like you should buy something; you enjoy, or are so numbed by the experience of shopping that you do it for its own sake almost as a ritual; shopping in a group is a social activity and makes you feel part of things; you desire things so much that you forget whether they are actually a priority use of your money; you may find you can get credit and that this somehow makes you feel you have lots of money to spend.

The golden rule in managing finances is to monitor your spending.

The National Youth Agency

Here are some suggestions for managing your account:

- as you spend keep the receipts (this includes cash machine and till receipts);
- always get a receipt from the cash machine;
- make a note of all cheques you write;
- keep a record of all the Switch or Delta payments you make;
- watch your standing orders and direct debits;
- at the end of every month tick off your payments against your standing order to confirm what you have spent;
- and, always check your bank statement carefully. Mistakes are surprisingly common.

The following points are adapted from *A Student's Guide to Better Money Management*, published by Credit Action an organisation which aims to help people manage their money better.

- To manage your money well you have to be completely honest with yourself. It is no good 'forgetting' how much money you spend in the pub or on magazines every week. These smaller amounts can add up and you may be surprised how much you actually do spend when you keep an eye on them.
- If you have regular money coming in (for example a benefit payment, income from work, or a student grant), try and plan how you will spend it over the period it is to last for. Don't be tempted to spend it all at once.
- Spend sensibly – remember that tomorrow's need is more important than today's want. To help plan your spending, write out a weekly or monthly budget plan.

■ The above information is from the National Youth Agency's web site www.youthinformation.com

© 2000 National Youth Agency

SIMON KNEEBONE

Banking

Information from *u*project

A bank account can help you to manage your money. It also saves you having to carry your cash with you wherever you go (or stashing it under the bed!).

There are three main types of bank account:

- basic bank account
- current account
- savings account.

Basic bank account

This is sometimes called an introductory bank account. They are designed to be simple and easy to set up. All of the banks offering basic bank accounts provide a cashpoint card. This lets you get money out of any cash machine that accepts your card, as long as there is enough money in your account. To do this you will need to type in your PIN (Personal Identification Number). Some banks also provide a debit card, which means that you can use it in shops to buy things, as long as you have enough money in your account. You can use a bank account to set up direct debits, so you can pay regular bills straight from your account – but you need to make sure that you have enough money in your account to cover any direct debits you set up (visit www.directdebit.co.uk)

Because basic bank accounts are designed to be simple, they usually do not provide chequebooks. This means that you can't go overdrawn by writing cheques when you don't have enough money in your account. But with some accounts you do get a buffer zone. This means, for instance, that if you have £9 in your account you can still withdraw a £10 note from the cashpoint – so you'll have a very small overdraft until you next pay money in.

Basic bank accounts are good for people who might have difficulty getting a current account, for instance because they have a low income or because they have had problems paying off loans in the past. They are also good for those who

want to avoid getting an overdraft or those who need to manage their money carefully.

A number of banks provide basic bank accounts. With some banks the minimum age for opening a basic bank account is 16, with others it is 18. No minimum balance (first amount you pay in) is required to open a basic bank account.

Current account

You have to be 16 or over to open a current account. It's called a current account because people use it for day-to-day (current) things like paying in their wages, paying bills and taking money out for shopping and going out.

If you open a current account you will get a cashpoint card which you can use at cash machines. You will also get a chequebook. This means you can pay for some things by cheque – for example any bill that is sent to your home address. But when you're out and about you'll find that most places won't accept a cheque unless you've got a cheque guarantee card, which is set at a

---

If you're opening a current account, it's worth shopping around to find out which one suits you best

---

certain limit (for example £50). This means that you can write a cheque in a shop for up to £50 and the shop assistant will accept it because the bank has guaranteed that they will cash the cheque. Because this system can lead to people writing cheques even though they don't have the money in their account, you usually have to be with your bank for a little while before they will give you a cheque guarantee card. This makes sense for you and for the bank – it stops you getting into debt and it stops the bank losing money on customers who can't pay back their debts.

If you're opening a current account, it's worth shopping around to find out which one suits you best. You might want to go to the bank that has a branch close to where you live. Or, if you have access to the internet, you might want to go to a bank that lets you access your account on-line. This means you can check your balance or make bill payments whenever you want to. Most banks also offer a telephone banking service, but it's worth checking exactly what you can and can't do by phone.

There are some other things you should check before you open a bank account:

- that there are no one-off or regular charges for everyday transactions (like using cheques, or sending you statements which tell you

- what's happening in your account)
- that you can pay cash and cheques in at your branch (or at a convenient cashpoint)
- that you can set up direct debits and standing orders
- that you are getting the lowest charges on overdrafts. Some banks will give you an overdraft to an agreed limit and will charge you interest, but no extra fee. Others charge a fee on top. Make sure you don't go overdrawn without agreeing the limit first, as the charges can be very high.

Savings account

If you can put aside some money – even just a bit – it really is worth thinking about getting a savings account. Money put in your savings account will earn you higher interest rates than money hanging around in a current account. This means that your money will grow by a certain percentage (the 'interest rate') even when you are not paying into the account.

If you have got a savings account and you are a taxpayer, you will be taxed on any interest you are paid, because it is a form of income. So if you are saving on a regular basis and don't need immediate access to your money, you might want to consider opening an Individual Savings Account (ISA). There are a number of different kinds of ISA but the most straightforward is a Cash ISA. With a Cash ISA the money you make in interest is paid to you tax-free, so you end up saving more.

- The above information is from *moneychoices* – a financial awareness activity pack developed for *u*project sponsored by Barclays. Visit the web site at www.uproject.org.uk

© Barclays Bank PLC 2002

Earn as you learn?

The average student these days leaves university between £10,000 and £20,000 in the red. What can you do to ease the pain, both now and later? John Crace reports

There's a downside to most things, and the downside to higher education is, inevitably, money. At the end of your three or four years at university, either you or your parents are going to be substantially poorer; and the chances are, if your parents aren't either generous or loaded, it's going to be you. The average student will leave university owing at least £10,000.

You'll pick up your debt in a number of ways. First, there's your tuition fees, which currently clock in at £1,100 a year (except in Scotland, where no fees are paid). If your parents earn less than £17,615 a year, you will be exempt. If they earn between £17,615 and £26,055 there's a sliding scale of contribution. Anything over that and you are liable for the whole lot, regardless of whether your parents give you the money or not. So, as you can see, it is likely to pay to stay on the right side of your parents. You may have been dying to leave home for years, but you've still got to be nice about it.

Most of your debt will come from living expenses, such as accommodation and food. Take it from me, fridges don't automatically fill themselves. How much you will owe by the time you graduate depends a great deal on where you choose to study.

The cost of living in London is much higher than in other parts of the country, and this is reflected in the student loan allocations. If you are living away from home in London you can apply for up to £4,815 a year, while those out of the capital are entitled to a maximum of £3,905.

There is one easy way to reduce your debt: live at home. How much you will be asked to contribute towards your upkeep is then a matter of negotiation between you and your parents, but as the maximum student loan available to those at home is £3,090, you can see you're in line for a big reduction. Whether you want to live at home is another matter. For many students, part of the attraction of going to university is about discovering new places and claiming their independence. But it comes with a price tag.

This, of course, may only be the start. Many students rack up higher debts than this. Once their loan has disappeared, many high street banks are only too happy to lend students a few thousand pounds more – at normal commercial rates of interest, unlike student loans.

It's about now that you're probably regretting that you weren't born a few years earlier, when tuition fees were non-existent and there were still maintenance grants available. If so, you should really be counting yourself lucky you aren't three years younger, as in 2006 the government plans to allow universities to increase tuition fees to £3,000 a year.

Higher education is in a financial black hole. Roderick Floud, the president of Universities UK, reckons the sector needs £10bn to redress the erosion of investment over the past 25 years and to make our universities competitive with those elsewhere – the US in particular. The National Union of Students (NUS) has called for the government to fund this out of general taxation, but the chances of this happening are substantially less than nil. Even before the war with Iraq and the worldwide economic recession left Gordon Brown with a forecast shortfall of roughly £20bn, the government was unwilling to fund the entire higher education deficit.

Which is why you are having to pay and why it is important that you should plan your university career carefully. As a general rule of thumb, graduates tend to earn more than those without degrees and the simplistic financial equation suggests that the value of the qualification – not to mention the fun to be had over the period of the course – more than offsets the debt. But there are short-term variables that need to be

How much debt can students expect to come out of uni with? Barclays' Student Debt Survey 2000 estimates £6,507. However, as these are students who may have received a part grant with their support, Barclays estimates that graduate will have a debt of about £10,000 in summer 2001 (a 54 per cent rise on 2000).

	NUS Hardship Survey	Barclays' Graduate Survey 2000	Calculation	Total for 3 years
Loan	52%	79%	£3,815 (£4,700 in London)	£11,445 (£14,300 in London)
Overdraft	54.7%	60%	£2,000 (usual amount available)	£2,000
Credit card	27.8%	29%	£500 (usual limit available)	£500
Family	4.2%	12%	1,300 (average loan expected NUS Hardship Survey)	£1,300
Total				£15,245

Source: National Union of Students (NUS)

added in. Especially if you are applying through Clearing.

With the disappointment of not having been accepted by your first choices, combined with the feeling that you have to do something quickly now if you want to go to university this year, it can be tempting to accept the first offer that comes along.

But think before you jump. There will almost certainly be a university somewhere that will offer you a place to study something. Many universities are as strapped for cash as you are; the government wants 50% of young people to be in higher education by 2010 and the institutions are under pressure to deliver this target.

The amount of cash that each university gets from the Higher Education Funding Council for England is partly determined by the number of students it has on roll. So there will be a few universities that will be eager to fill some of their less popular courses and will be anxious for your business. But before you accept, remember that your decision will have financial as well as academic implications. If it turns out you don't like either the university or the course and choose to leave after the first year, you're likely to be about £5,000 out of pocket with nothing to show for it.

But let's assume you've chosen wisely. Now what? Most students will take some form of job to help pay their way; for some this may be evening bar work or shifts in McDonald's, but an increasing number will be in full-time employ-ment. Recent research by the University of Hertfordshire shows one in five students holds down a full-time job and a further one in 10 clocks up a 50-hour work/study week – exceeding the recommended hours set by the government's working time directive.

In other words, the days of students loafing around all day are by and large over. While an eight-hour day is normal in the workplace, for many students it's just the start: 56% put in up to 20 hours of paid work a week on top of their educa-tion. The idea of combining full-time employment with a full-time education may be semantically challenging, but for some it's a reality.

There are knock-on problems. One in 10 students have fallen asleep during lectures, 12% have bunked off lectures to be at work and a further one in 10 say they choose course modules to fit in with their work schedules. Another survey carried out for Universities UK last year found that 43% of students occasionally produced poor-quality assignments as a result of having to undertake paid employment, and 80% said their paid work reduced the time available for reading and working independently.

'For many, the experience of working whilst at university is a good one, but some find it difficult to juggle both'

These, then, are the hard facts, and, despite the pressures, nothing much is likely to give. Indeed, increasingly both students and universities have been attempting to make a virtue of a vice. One in three students believes that paid employ-ment gives them important experience for their CV that will stand them in good stead after graduation. Others find even more immediate benefits: 42% say that paid work enables them to organise their time better and 28% say it motivates them to apply themselves to their studies.

David Ball, dean of students at University of Hertfordshire, says: 'Our research dispels the myth that students have an easy ride. Nowadays it is almost inevitable that most will take on a part-time job and this can be a great way of enhancing their employability once they graduate.

'For many, the experience of working whilst at university is a good one, but some find it difficult to juggle both – and their studies can often suffer as a result. It's a question of finding the right balance between the two and it is universities' responsibility to help students find that balance.'

To make life easier, many universities enable students to access some or all of their coursework online.

If, after all this, you are still not so keen on the working student life, you have one further option. Following the Cubie report, Scotland did away with upfront tuition fees back in 1999. Don't all head north of the border at once.

■ This article first appeared in *The Guardian*, 14 August 2003.

© *John Crace*

Banks

Information from PUSH

If you treat it right, a student bank account can be like a little pot of gold at the end of the rainbow. A very little pot of gold, admittedly, and they'll want the money back eventually, but in the meantime they're very handy.

Most banks suck up to students like they were millionaires (because they hope one day that's exactly what they'll be – or, at any rate, they know they're likely to be richer than non-graduates). To entice students to open accounts, banks offer them freebies, good deals and, more importantly, free overdrafts.

Banks, however, have more patience with some students than with others, and it's not all down to how nice you are. They cut medical students quite a bit of slack, for instance, letting them run up debts like mice run up clocks. It makes economic sense to them, because those students are more likely to be safe bets financially.

Not that banks are actually mean to the others. It's just that most students are scared of talking to their bank because they owe them so much money, and they know the bank has the power to cut off their cash supply. And the less you talk to your bank, especially when you think things may get tight, the more likely they are to get shirty with you when they actually do.

Overdrafts

An overdraft is a minus amount of money in your account. So an 'overdraft limit' is the sum that your bank has decided you're allowed to take out of your account even though you haven't actually got any money in there.

Most banks offer a free overdraft facility to students up to a certain limit. So long as you don't go over the limit, you won't get slapped with charges for most day-to-day banking stuff and they won't charge you any interest on what you borrow – one of those rare times when someone'll lend you money without wanting back more than you borrowed in the first place.

Depending on your year of study, the overdraft limit is usually between £750 and £2,000 (it grows as your student debts accumulate). If there's any danger that you're not going to be able to stick to the limit, you need to have a chat with your bank's student adviser to arrange an 'extension'. They may charge you interest, they may even charge you a

---

Banks, however, have more patience with some students than with others, and it's not all down to how nice you are

---

fee for extending the overdraft at all, but it'll be a lot less than they'd have charged you if you hadn't got their say-so in the first place.

A couple of don'ts

Don't wait till you're nearly at you limit before trying to arrange an extension, 'cos then you're stuffed if they say no. And don't exceed your limit without getting authorisation to do so. Your overdraft is then no longer free, and you get hit with charges and fines. There'll be fines for going over the limit and for bouncing cheques (ie. not honouring them), and they'll even charge you for sending you a letter to tell you that you're over your limit. Then they'll fine you because you can't pay the charges.

Worst of all, they'll charge interest. Interest rates on un-authorised overdrafts can be huge. You'd call it criminal, if an un-authorised overdraft wasn't basically taking their money without asking first. So if you get stung, remember who started it.

While you're a student, your bank overdraft is the cheapest and easiest way of borrowing – cheaper even than student loans, because there's literally no interest on most

authorised student overdrafts while student loans rack up interest from day one.

However, overdrafts do have to be paid back eventually, and the bank theoretically has the right to ask for the money at any time. After you've graduated, most start charging interest (although often not immediately) and it doesn't take long for overdrafts to become an expensive form of amusement. So don't get complacent about your overdraft – it's certainly a lifeline for most students, but it's not an automatic right.

Deferment period

Slim Jim the Fence owes Joey the Knife $10,000. Joey gives him three days to come up with the money – that's a 'deferment period'.

To put it another way, it's a period of time that a bank gives you either to raise the funds to repay an overdraft or loan or, more usually, to find work. When banks offer a deferment period, it tends to be more by way of a practical approach to debt management rather than a threat (as it is with Joey the Knife).

Don't get complacent about your overdraft – it's certainly a lifeline for most students, but it's not an automatic right

---

Rather than immediately snatching every penny you earn and landing you in as much financial crap as you endured as a student, a deferment period helps you settle into a job and ease your way into repayments. Banks usually give students a year or two (or even three) after they've graduated before giving them a hard time about repaying their overdraft.

If a bank doesn't offer a deferment period to graduates, you may want to look elsewhere.

Picking a bank

Faced with the fountain of freebies and the glut of goodies on offer from

every high street bank, it's almost as hard to choose a bank as it is to choose a university.

They nearly all provide online and telephone banking services, and most offer interest-fee prearranged overdrafts, preferential rates on loans, and probably staff who'll perform sexual favours.

Don't get suckered by the gimmicks. It's worth shopping around to get the best banking deal you can.

Before deciding, you should get answers to the following questions:

- How much interest will you get on money in your account for the short period that you happen to be in credit (usually that's only for a few weeks after getting your first student loan instalment)? The interest is often so small you can't even fold it.
- What's your maximum overdraft limit? And check it's interest-free.
- How quickly do they expect you to pay off your debts and when?
- How nasty are the charges levied for unauthorised overdrafts? They will be nasty, but some are the stuff of nightmares.
- What are the facilities like, such as the number and location of cash machines? Is there or will there be a cash machine near where you go every day as a student (either on campus or wherever you're living)?
- Is there a branch somewhere convenient?
- If you can't get to a branch when it's open, what other banking

services do they offer – such as over the phone or on the internet? What can and can't you do by phone or online?
- Do they charge anything if you use another bank's cash machine and if so how much?
- Do they offer specialist advice for students and graduates?
- How easy is it to set up and cancel standing orders and direct debits?
- If you care, how sound are they? For example, do they have shady connections in other countries propping up dictatorships that abuse human rights?
- What freebies do you get and what are they really worth to you?

Don't get suckered by the gimmicks. It's worth shopping around to get the best banking deal you can

---

- Do they offer student bank loans beyond overdrafts and on what terms?
- What support will they give you once you've graduated?

■ The above information is from PUSH's web site which can be found at www.push.co.uk

© Push 2003

Managing money

Information from *u*project

Budgeting

The starting point for managing your money is to have a budget. This is just a plan for how you are going to spend the money that you have. The top tips for good budgeting are:

1. Make sure you know how much money you've got coming in.
2. Put money aside for what you need, before you buy things you want.
3. Spend less than you earn, and you'll never go over budget.

If you're finding it hard to make ends meet, see if any of these help:

- Is there anywhere you can make savings?
  – can you make your own lunch instead of buying sandwiches?
  – can you go shopping at cheaper shops?
- Make sure that you're not spending money on unnecessary things:
  – if you have a bank account, make sure you're not being charged for basic services
  – if you've got a mobile phone, are you on the best deal?
  – if you have to pay bills, try to do it on direct debit as it's usually cheaper
  – food shopping can often be cheaper at local streetmarkets than supermarkets.

- Think very carefully before getting a credit card or store card – if you use one you will be spending money that you don't currently have, and probably paying interest.
- Each week, however hard it is, try to save a little bit
  – this will give you a safety net if you need extra cash in a hurry.
- If you're planning on moving away from home, remember it can be expensive
  – work out how much money you are likely to need. The most expensive things will probably be rent, food and bills. But don't forget things like going out, travel and mobile phone calls.

Credit

You have to be over 18 to apply for any form of credit. Here's a quick guide to how it works. Credit can come in the form of:

- bank overdrafts and bank loans

Spend less than you earn, and you'll never go over budget

- credit cards and store cards (these are a kind of credit card)
- hire-purchase schemes and catalogues
- interest-free credit (for instance in electrical shops).

How do you get credit?

First of all, you need to have a good credit history. This usually means that you need to have a bank account, that you have regular money coming in and that you can manage your money.

What are the advantages?

Credit is useful if you need to buy something quickly. This might be because it's an emergency, or it might be because you've seen a fantastic bargain you don't want to miss out on. Because you usually pay credit back in monthly instalments, if you use it really carefully it can help with managing your budget, because you don't have to pay for something all at once.

What are the disadvantages?

Credit can tempt you to spend money you don't have, or can't afford to pay back. Don't ever take out credit on the spur of the moment and make sure you have a plan for paying it

SIMON KNEEBONE

back. And remember that you usually have to pay interest, which makes things more expensive. If you buy a TV for £100 and the company charges you 15% interest over one year, you will end up paying £115 in total.

Different rates of interest

The interest you have to pay will vary depending on the rate charged (this is known as the 'Annual Percentage Rate' or APR). All types of loans have an APR and you need to keep your eyes open to get the best deal:

- a bank overdraft you have arranged will have a lower APR than one that hasn't been authorised;
- a credit card will probably have a higher APR than a bank loan.

Financial Health Warning!

Credit can be tempting – and sometimes the less money you have, the more tempting it is. For some people, this can end up in a spiral where they are spending a lot of money paying off old credit bills – and then have to pay for new things on credit because they've got no cash left. The other temptation is to borrow money from people like 'loan sharks' to pay off your credit – but they can charge you a lot of interest. So take care!

Debt

If you owe money to friends and family, the bank, or a credit company, and you can't afford to pay it back, face up to your debt immediately. First, work out how you have got into debt. Is it because:

You've had to spend a lot of money on a one-off item (like a mobile phone bill that got out of control)?
Try to make a deal with the people you owe money to. If it's a bill of some kind, ask if you can pay off a fixed amount each month.

Try to pay by direct debit – this means the money goes out of your bank account automatically.

You've regularly been spending too much on smaller items (like CDs or cigarettes)?
Chances are this kind of debt has crept up on you. Do a proper budget for the future and try to stick to it.

If you've run into debt with the bank or credit company, talk to them as soon as possible to explain the situation. Be prepared in advance with a plan to pay back what you owe.

You just don't have enough to buy the basics to live on?

If you can't pay for basic living costs and this is serious risk to your health or safety, you can apply for a Crisis Loan. This is an interest-free loan from the government that you have to pay back – the amount you can get will depend on your circumstances. Before the money is given to you, you have to agree how you will pay it back.

Don't be tempted to borrow money from an unauthorised money lender ('loan shark'). They charge very high interest rates and will probably end up making your debt problem worse.

It might help to talk through your situation with someone – perhaps your Connexions Personal Adviser or a youth worker. They might recommend that you speak to a money expert.

Banking

A bank account can help you to manage your money. It also saves you having to carry your cash with you wherever you go (or stashing it under the bed!).

There are three main types of bank account.
- Basic bank account
- Current account
- Savings account

Basic bank account

You should think about getting a basic bank account if:
- You have difficulty getting a current account
- You don't want to be able to go overdrawn

With a basic bank account you should get:
- A cashpoint card and PIN number
- The option to set up direct debits
- A 'buffer zone' – so for example if you have less than £10 in your account, you can still withdraw £10 from a cashpoint. Not all banks offer this, so check the small print.

You will need to be 16 or 18 to open an account (check with individual banks).

Current account

You should think about getting a current account if:
- You want a cheque book and cheque guarantee card
- You want to get an overdraft facility

With a current account you should get:
- A cashpoint card and PIN number
- a debit card to pay for things in shops, by phone and online
- a cheque book (but you may have to be with the bank for a while before you get a guarantee card)
- the option to set up direct debits

You usually have to be 16 or over and pass the bank credit check to get all the services associated with a current account. Online and telephone banking are now available at many banks.

Savings account

You should think about getting a savings account if:
- you want to put some money away that you won't be touching for a while

The key features are:
- Higher interest rates – so your money grows even when you're not paying in
- If you're a taxpayer you can open a Cash ISA which means that you won't have to pay tax on your savings. Check to see the range on offer.

- The above information is from *moneychoices* – a financial awareness activity pack developed for *u*project sponsored by Barclays. Visit the web site at www.uproject.org.uk

© Barclays Bank PLC 2002

Credit can be tempting – and sometimes the less money you have, the more tempting it is

Ten tips for cutting debt

By Chris Tryhorn

1. Get advice

If you have problem with debt, you're far from alone; Citizens' Advice Bureaux deal with over a million cases a year. They, the Consumer Credit Counselling Service (CCCS) and National Debt Line all dispense free advice – you don't need to rush to pay for support, as stiff fees will often only add to your debt in the short term.

2. Acknowledge the problem early – don't wait until it's too late

The CCCS reckons that if your repayments (excluding mortgages) reach 20% of your net income, you have a problem – facing up to this is a major step in the right direction. Once you are locked into a ruthlessly money-saving mentality, you can get into the right habits. That means curbing your wilder instincts, and not splashing out on anything before you've really thought through if you can afford it.

3. Pay off debts before you spend

Keep it simple: more money in than out means that you'll have freedom to manoeuvre, so get into the habit of clearing the decks monthly. Paying for things outright is better than paying on credit, unless you can manage delayed payments reliably. In this way, debit cards can be a better option.

Keep it simple: more money in than out means that you'll have freedom to manoeuvre, so get into the habit of clearing the decks monthly

4. Consolidation?

It is tempting to simplify your repayments by consolidating, or lumping them all together. But beware of secured loans, which are often the ones cheerily advertised on daytime television. Their genial reminders that your home could be at risk if you do not keep up repayments should not be treated lightly.

5. Be honest and communicate with creditors

Debt is a common problem, and creditors are used to working with people – it's in their interest to reclaim your money. It's better to stay in touch with the debt rather than evading the issue, says Amy Brown of the CCCS. She advises: 'Keep making a token payment, even £1 a month – it shows good faith and makes it easier in the future if you do end up in court.'

6. Sort out your expenses

You may be spending money on things that are far from essential. Draw up a list of priority payments and grant yourself an emergency allowance on top of what you think is essential – 10% is recommended by the National Association of Citizens' Advice Bureaux (NACAB). This can then be drawn on when unforeseen expenses nibble into your budget. Remember that blowouts like Christmas can play havoc with your good intentions.

7. Get a grip on your credit rating

You need to have a clear idea of your financial status. Details of your credit rating, which affect your ability to qualify for loans, are held by the two agencies Experian and Equifax, and you can access them for a small fee.

8. Shop around for credit cards

It's so easy to put it all on the plastic, and there are some good deals out there. So make sure you don't end up paying over the odds; some store cards can charge you interest rates of around 30% a year. Shopping around generally for financial services and asserting yourself as a consumer will strengthen your control over your situation. The best loan and credit card rates can be found at moneysupermarket.co.uk.

9. Repay more than the minimum

Don't fall into the trap of making do with the minimum repayment. NACAB suggests clearing at least 10% of your credit card balance every month. And 'payment holidays' in credit card or loan arrangements will come at the cost of interest.

10. Take care judging a loan's terms

Monthly payments are not the whole story. It's important to calculate the total amount you must repay: although a loan's instalments may appear low, over the course of the repayment you may build up a steeper overall bill. The picture is complicated when loans have variable interest rates and this is something you should bear in mind.

© Guardian Newspapers Limited 2003

Credit cards

Information from www.plasticmoney.org.uk

You can use credit cards to make payments when buying things and to withdraw cash. There is a maximum limit to the amount of money you can spend with a credit card. This is called the credit limit. It is arranged with the bank or issuer of the card. Different people have different credit limits and they can be raised or lowered when circumstances change.

Whenever you buy something with your card, the sale or transaction is recorded. At the end of each month, you receive a statement listing everything you've bought over that period. You must always repay a minimum amount of the bill each month – usually 3-5 per cent of the total.

The money which you have still to pay back is called the amount outstanding. It is up to you whether you pay off more than the minimum amount.

Interest is charged on all transactions if you don't repay the full amount by a certain date.

Gold and Platinum cards are cards which normally have a higher credit limit (minimum £3,000) and a higher annual fee than credit cards

Normally, this will be about 25 days after you've received the statement but the details vary with each issuer. Some cards also have an annual fee of between £10-£12.

Gold and Platinum cards are cards which normally have a higher credit limit (minimum £3,000) and a higher annual fee than credit cards. They are used by people who use their cards a lot or who want to make expensive purchases.

Most credit cards, except the store cards offered by larger shops and supermarkets, are linked to one of the three international card payment schemes – American Express, MasterCard or Visa.

These companies are responsible for maintaining the payment system technology behind plastic cards. They work closely with the card issuers. This means that you can use your card anywhere in the world where you see the signs for these firms. The signs are usually stuck on shop doors. They can also be found at the till or in advertisements.

■ The above information is from Credit Card Research Group's web site which can be found at www.plasticmoney.org.uk

© Credit Card Research Group

Storing up trouble

We've proved it's all too easy to take out store cards, but, as most charge around 30 per cent a year in interest, there's a nasty sting in the tail, says Robert Watts

Every day, thousands of shoppers queuing to pay for goods at tills up and down the land are asked whether they would like to save 10 per cent on the purchase price. The more honest question would be: 'Do you want to sign up for a credit card which charges nearly three times as much as many conventional cards?'

Store cards are big business. There are 21 million in issue, compared with 8 million 10 years ago. Consumer groups have long complained about the hard sell used to get people to sign up, often by poorly trained staff who are typically paid commission or given sales targets.

Both Experian and Equifax, the country's two largest credit reference agencies, insisted last week that someone making a series of applications in quick succession over a couple of hours would normally be picked up quickly and the applications blocked.

'Each time someone applies for credit, their reference is flagged,' says Neil Munroe, director of external affairs at Equifax. 'The system is pretty secure. The idea that someone could wander down a high street taking out a batch of credit cards, well, it's just extremely unlikely.'

But that is exactly what Claire Packham did. Claire is a 20-year-old student with £5,000 worth of student loan debt. In a little under two hours last week, she managed to amass instant credit of £1,600 on five store cards, often with only a debit card as ID.

When shoppers apply for a store card, their credit rating is checked with one of the credit reference agencies – though not immediately, if Claire's experience is typical. At a time when identity theft is soaring, her story raises serious questions about the selling of store cards and the gaps in credit checking systems.

'Shoppers are dazzled by the discounts,' says Frances Harrison of the National Consumer Council. 'What they often fail to realise is that any initial saving is quickly eaten up by the steep interest charges on the cards.'

'Don't borrow on a store card,' is the blunt advice from Melanie Green of the Consumers' Association. 'Even the most expensive credit cards are usually better value. If you've built a balance on one of these cards, switch it to a normal credit card or, better, take out a personal loan.'

While the standard annual percentage rate (APR) on most store cards is about 30 per cent, you can pay around seven per cent on a personal loan, and many ordinary credit cards charge standard rates as low as 10 per cent. John Lewis's store card and Tesco's credit card charge only 13 per cent.

The Consumers' Association calculates that the difference in cost can be staggering. Interest at seven per cent on a £5,000 personal loan over three years totals £540. Interest over the same period on the same

sum on a store card with an APR of 30 per cent would be £2,302.

Members of the Treasury Select Committee were deeply critical of the rates charged when they investigated store cards a few weeks ago. 'You all seem to be charging around 28 to 30 per cent, which rather suggests you are running a nice cosy cartel,' said George Mudie, the Labour MP, while James Plaskitt, MP for Warwick and Leamington, dubbed GE Consumer Finance a 'designer loan-shark'.

When we asked River Island, Wallis and Bhs why Claire was able to obtain so much instant credit in their stores, all three refused to answer, referring us to GE Capital, the vast US bank that runs their card accounts.

GE told us that its procedures had functioned as normal in Claire's case. But it added that student loans did not show up on credit agency files.

So why are its rates so high? The company would only say: 'The interest rate is reflective of the total cost of running the programme, not just the current cost of the funds.'

GE confirmed that staff are paid a 'small reward' for each store card they arrange, but would not detail the size of commission, adding that it varies from retailer to retailer.

Liz Piner, the retail director of French Connection, replied herself, rather than hide behind the Royal Bank of Scotland, which manages the FCUK card account. But she offered little more than platitudes such as: 'We see our cards not as an invitation to take out credit, but as a loyalty scheme.'

Piner admits staff are set card sales targets, but says they are rewarded with vouchers and hampers rather than cash.

French Connection would not say why credit cards sold through its stores by RBS carry an APR nearly twice the size of those sold directly by the bank, which have an APR of 14.9 per cent.

© *Telegraph Group Limited, London 2003*

Managing your money

Information from the National Union of Students (NUS)

More and more opportunities for debt and credit are offered to students (for example, through loans, overdrafts and credit cards), so it is imperative that students are aware of the pitfalls as well as the advantages and temptations of the many different sources of income. Mismanaging debt may have serious implications legally as well as financially. This article offers some tips for managing your money and managing debt.

1. Money management support

Many college student services and/or students' union welfare services offer money management and debt counselling services. NUS would advise prospective and existing students to make use of these services either before or early in their course to boost money management skills. Some basic strategies for money management are outlined below.

a. Find out about living and study costs.

Research has indicated that both further and higher education students tend to underestimate the real costs of study and living. For example a recent survey by NOP on behalf of Goldfish found that around 50% of sixth formers underestimated or had no idea of the costs of going to university. Common areas of under-estimation include hidden course costs and travel costs. NUS provides national estimates of costs for one year of study for full-time under-graduates. However, institutions or students' unions often provide estimates of local living and study costs. Make sure you contact your intended place of study to help you plan realistically for expenses.

> *Mismanaging debt may have serious implications legally as well as financially*

b. Budgeting

Work out what income you have and what you will have to spend (each month, for example). The institution should have student advisers in the students' union and/or the college who can help with this. This will help you to work out if you need more money. You may want to complete a budget planner such as the one included in this article.

Make sure you know how your income will be paid. For example, if you get a student loan, you may get three instalments over your year of study. However, if you receive an NHS bursary you will be paid monthly.

c. Record keeping

Make sure you keep up-to-date records of your income, spending and sources of debt. Your college or students' union may be able to help you to set up records and monitor your records.

d. Understand your entitlements

Make sure you know what funding you are entitled to and what else you may be able to apply for in terms of student support, for example Access or Hardship Funds (see NUS Information Sheet 14) and other college funds or charitable sources (see NUS Information Sheet 10 for 'alternative funding' sources). Make sure you make the most of discounts available to you, such as those available through using the NUS Card and www.nusonline.co.uk.

e. Coping with debt

If you find that you are not managing your finances, but your finances are managing you – seek advice from your institution, your students' union, your local Citizens' Advice

Bureau. They may help you with prioritising your debts, corresponding with creditors and managing a budget.

2. Banking

a. Student accounts

Banks tend to offer specific preferential services to full-time undergraduates. Students on courses of further education and postgraduate education may find it more difficult to secure preferential services such as interest-free overdrafts or higher-rate cheque guarantee cards. However, a few banks are catching onto this, particularly within the 16-19 age range. Important points to stress are:

- Shop around for the best offer for you (for example some students may want £35 as an incentive for opening an account, whereas others may prefer retail discounts).

- Check the interest rates on your account, both for an account in credit and for an unauthorised overdraft. The latter can often be extremely high and best to avoid.

- Check the availability of the branches near your intended place of study and whether the bank has a specific Student Officer available. Having a face-to-face staff officer who understands the needs of students often helps when you are facing particular problems (e.g. your grant/loan cheque hasn't arrived on time).

- Try to open a bank account before starting college – you will avoid the crush and save time in getting access to the services and to your money.

- In your final year of study check what will happen to your account when you graduate. Some banks will offer graduate accounts, which may be worth considering.

The Support 4 Learning website contains a regularly updated summary of student bank account offers – www.support4learning.org.uk.

b. Graduate accounts

Many banks now offer graduate accounts, which allow graduating students a period of interest-free overdraft and/or a preferential rate on loans. Make sure that you check

Student expenditure		
NUS estimated average student expenditure for academic year 2002/03 (39 weeks)		
	Average expenditure	
	Inside London	**Outside London**
Course costs:		
Tuition fees	£1,100	£1,100
Other fees	£14	£14
Books/equip. etc.	£367	£367
Photocopying	£36	£36
Sub-total:	£1,517	£1,517
Living costs:		
Rent	£2,814	£2,003
Utility bills	£394	£394
Food/household goods	£1,043	£1,043
Laundry	£104	£104
Insurance	£76	£61
Clothing	£394	£394
Travel	£709	£452
Leisure	£1,349	£1,349
Sub-total:	£6,883	£5,800
Total	**£8,400**	**£7,317**
Potential income		
Loan (for 39 week period – excludes amount for long vacation)	£3611	£2929
Shortfall	**£4789**	**£4388**

Source: National Union of Students (NUS)

the conditions linked to these accounts, for example, what is the maximum interest-free overdraft offered? What will happen to your outstanding overdraft? When will the interest-free period end, and what happens then? Can you merge a number of debts? Some banks will allow you to open a graduate account with preferential overdraft and loan rates without you having held a student account with them. Check www.support4learning.org.uk for conditions.

3. Sources of income

a. Student support

As stated in section 1, ensure you know what support you are entitled to (i.e.: statutory support) and what support you may get if you meet the eligibility criteria (i.e. discretionary support). NUS provides a range of information sheets covering both. Sources of discretionary support may

include Access or Hardship Funds (see Information Sheet 14) or educational charities or trusts (see Information Sheet 10).

b. Paid work

The NUS Student Hardship Survey (1999) found that 41% of full-time undergraduates sampled undertook paid work during periods of study. The average hours of work were 13 per week and average pay was £4.53 per hour.

The TUC's 'Students at Work' Survey found that 60% of those students questioned had to work to meet basic living costs. If you are considering working whilst studying, it is worth thinking about your options – e.g. does the college/students' union run an employment agency? This way, you may be guaranteed at least the minimum wage. The minimum wage is as follows:

	From 1 Oct 2001	From 1 Oct 2002
Development rate (18-21 year olds)	£3.50	£3.60
Main rate (22 years old and over)	£4.10	£4.20

What is the average wage for your area? What type of work is available in your area (i.e. shift work, evenings, weekends)? What hours will fit into your pattern of studies? Is there union representation within the workplace to protect your health and safety and employment rights?

c. Using credit

If you are using credit – for example, a credit card, store card or buying from a catalogue – check the interest rates and repayment conditions. Commercial lending often incurs severe penalties if borrowers don't keep to the repayment terms, so make sure you know what you are getting yourself into and try to use these sources as a last resort. If you are using credit, keep an eye on what you are using such credit for. For example, if you are using your credit card to pay for your food then it is likely that you need to seek financial advice and/or additional financial support from your institution.

Sources of Expenditure

a. Course costs

'Hidden' course costs – i.e. those costs not covered by upfront tuition fees – are an increasing cost for students. Find out how much a course is likely to actually cost per year. Information should be available either within an institution's prospectus, from the course tutor or possibly from the students' union. Important points to include: are you required to buy a lot of equipment (e.g. Arts and Textiles, Engineering, Architecture courses)?

Monthly budget planner

Income £
Student loan
Grant
Contributions from family
Earnings
Other
Total
Total monthly income

Monthly expenditure £
Fixed outgoings
Rent/mortgage
Gas/electricity
Telephone (rental)
Water rates
Insurance
TV licence/rental
Other
Total
Variable outgoings
Travel costs
Books/stationery/photocopying
Telephone calls
Food/meals
Laundry
Clothing
Toiletries
Sports/hobbies/leisure
Club/society subscriptions
Occasional costs (e.g. holidays, presents etc.)
Other
Total
Total monthly expenditure

Monthly budget £
Monthly income
Minus total outgoings
Total monthly budget

What books will you need? Are you required to photocopy study packs/books and how much will this cost

per term? Will you be required to attend field trips and how much will this cost per term? Then think about how you can save on these costs – Can you share books/equipment with other students? Can the institution help with the costs of equipment and books through the Access/Hardship Funds?

b. Living costs

NUS provides estimates of average living costs for an undergraduate during one year of study. This is useful as a guide, but will vary depending on the course requirements (books, equipment, field trips) and local costs of living. Find out the average costs for living near the college (your students' union or institution may provide estimates). This will help you decide whether you can afford to live and study in a specific area with the money you expect to have.

Whilst NUS has taken care to ensure that all information was accurate at the time of writing, readers are advised to check legislative provision before action.

NUS provides information on student finance and other student-related issues and can be contacted at: 461 Holloway Road, London N7 6LJ. Tel: 020 7272 8900. Website: www.nusonline.co.uk

■ The above information is from the National Union of Students. For more information visit their web site at www.nusonline.co.uk

© *National Union of Students (NUS)*

Student debt

Information from the Consumer Credit Counselling Service

A dedicated helpline for students worried about debt and money problems has been set up by the UK's leading debt charity, the Consumer Credit Counselling Service (CCCS).

The aim, according to CCCS Chairman, Malcolm Hurlston, is to ensure that nobody gives up studying because of worries about debt. He says:

'There are indications that students are panicking about mounting debts and feel obliged to drop out and start earning "real money". Wherever possible, we want to prevent this and help everyone to reach their full potential.

'The loss of grants and the introduction of tuition fees puts particular pressures on today's students, but in the long run, graduates are likely to earn more than non-graduates. There is evidence that although debts are rising, so too are graduate starting salaries. The average graduate starting salary is £13,422 while many of those lucky enough to find work in London can earn between £20,000 and £25,000 in their first job. It would be a shame if any were to give up because of a lack of financial guidance.'

The CCCS, which helps over 100,000 people a year with debt problems, has trained a number of its counsellors to deal specifically with student debt. This includes a thorough understanding of Student Loans and other benefits to which students are entitled.

According to Mr Hurlston, any student's potential future earning needs to be taken into account when offering advice:

'Student debt is different in that there may well be no money to pay off debts for a number of years, but graduate salaries can increase very quickly. Creditors understand this.

'We need to balance helping students to fund their education without leaving them to start their working lives overburdened by debt.'

Mandy Telford, President of the National Union of Students (NUS), is all too aware of the problems of debt and hardship amongst students. NUS campaigns on behalf of over five million students across the UK for a fairer funding system to alleviate the problems of debt and break down the financial barriers that prohibit so many talented people from fulfilling their potential.

> ### 'There are indications that students are panicking about mounting debts and feel obliged to drop out and start earning "real money"'

She said: 'Debt and money worries are the greatest fears students have whilst at university and while we continue to campaign for a better deal for our members we need to explore every avenue to make life better for them whilst at university. The last thing we want is more students falling by the wayside because of the enormous cost of going to university. It is reassuring to know that there are experts on hand to help our members and we urge them not to keep their problems to themselves or let them get out of hand.'

The Student Debtline is available on 0800 328 1813. Lines are open 8am-8pm, Mon to Fri.

Examples of young people with debt problems

Below are some examples of young people who have recently sought help from the Consumer Credit Counselling Service. Although the circumstances described are very real, the names have been changed to protect the identities of those concerned.

Ian is aged 28. He is employed as a housing officer and earns £1,400 net a month. He got into debt while still a student. He was unemployed for a while after leaving college since when he has found it very difficult to sort out his finances. When he sought help from the CCCS, he owed more than £30,000 to 12 creditors. He is now on a Debt Management Plan (DMP) with the CCCS. At the moment he is paying £220 per month which means it will take him 12 years to pay off the debt. He believes that he will be able to increase his

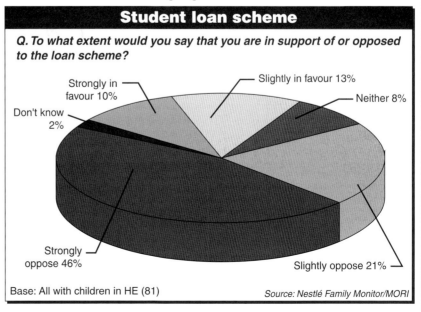

Student loan scheme

Q. To what extent would you say that you are in support of or opposed to the loan scheme?

- Strongly in favour 10%
- Slightly in favour 13%
- Neither 8%
- Don't know 2%
- Strongly oppose 46%
- Slightly oppose 21%

Base: All with children in HE (81)

Source: Nestlé Family Monitor/MORI

Debt and money worries are the greatest fears students have whilst at university

monthly payments once he has paid off his rent arrears.

Rachel is aged 26 and is employed as a personal assistant, earning £1,400 net per month. Since leaving university where she acquired a large number of debts she has continued to rely too much on credit and now owes £23,000 to seven different creditors. She started a DMP earlier this year which she plans to increase as soon as she has repaid some money she owes to her family.

■ If you are worried seek help from the Student Debtline on 0800 328 1813. This is run by the UK's leading debt charity, the Consumer Credit Counselling Service, and there is no charge for its services. Lines are open 8am-8pm Monday to Friday.

■ The above information is from the Consumer Credit Counselling Service's web site: www.cccs.co.uk

© Consumer Credit Counselling Service

Tips for students

1. Make sure that you obtain the entitlement which you need from the Student Loans company. You only get a chance to apply twice in each academic year. Check out what is available on its website on www.slc.co.uk.

2. If you get a job, make sure that you are paying the right tax. You can earn up to £4,615 without being taxed, so make sure your employer knows this and pays you correctly from the start. Get a P38 tax exemption form from your local tax office.

3. Budget. Boring but true – a budget plan before you go to university can really help. Write down all your expenditure: rent, bills, food and clothes, travel and of course socialising. Be realistic, then add 10 per cent to the total to cover unexpected costs. Will your income from grants, loans etc/ cover this? Do you need to think about a getting a job to help out?

4. Check out student bank accounts – you must have a bank account to receive a loan. Often banks offer attractive overdraft rates to students. Don't be swayed by gimmicky offers but choose the one which offers the best terms and conditions.

5. Check out bursaries. Finding out if you're eligible takes a lot of research. Some universities offer more than others, so check out what's available – your welfare officer or library should have the details. There are a number of directories which list bursaries that should be available at libraries. These are: *A Guide to University Scholarships and Awards* by Brian Heap (Trotman & Company), *The Educational Grants Directory* (published by the Directory of Social Change), *Scholarships for Students* (Hobsons) and *The Grants Register* (Macmillan).

6. Credit cards – be very wary of credit cards. Always look for the best rate and pay the minimum monthly payment at the very least. If you default on credit card payments now it means that you will have a bad credit record when you graduate, which can have serious implications – it could even affect your employability.

7. Travel off-peak whenever you can – fares are much lower. Remember to check out student discounts.

'There is a real need to upgrade financial literacy'

So says the chairman of a new group campaigning for extra education about money. Jenny Knight examines why it is needed

The British are woefully ignorant about their personal finances, according to the Consumers' Association.

Fewer than two in five consumers are confident about making their own financial decisions and only one in three has a clear idea of what financial products they need. More disconcertingly still, the numeracy skills of nearly half the adult population (48 per cent) were rated 'very poor' or 'poor' in a CA survey.

'There is a real need to upgrade financial literacy in this country,' says Ron Sandler, the new chairman of the Personal Finance Education Group (PFEG). 'My aim is to ensure that personal finance education in areas such as debt, savings, risk and returns, and basic skills like budgeting, is moved up the agenda.'

Sandler, whose Government-backed report on long-term savings was published last summer, adds: 'I have seen the consequences of people not really understanding the products

they were buying, and of not being able to discriminate between the good and the less good.'

PFEG, which supplies schools with teaching resources and specialist advisers, has helped personal finance gain a toehold in the National Curriculum. But teachers still have to battle to fit the subject into a tight timetable.

Mick Woodhouse of Rhodesway School in Bradford says: 'There's great scope for looking at financial products like endowment mortgages,

Items bought in the last week

Q. During the last 7 days, have you spent any of your own money on the following items?

	Alcoholic drinks	Arcade gambling	Books	Cigarettes	Clothes and footwear	Comics, magazines	Computer games	Cosmetics/ toiletries	Crisps	Discos or clubs	Fares	Fast food	Fresh fruit
Year 6 Male	4	*	13	1	*	26	38	*	31	14	*	*	*
Year 6 Female	1	*	20	1	*	36	12	*	29	16	*	*	*
Year 8 Male	5	7	4	3	8	19	17	3	25	9	11	23	7
Year 8 Female	4	2	5	5	23	29	3	18	27	14	17	21	7
Year 10 Male	18	8	3	11	18	21	16	5	29	13	21	34	6
Year 10 Female	20	2	4	18	29	29	2	30	29	19	31	29	6

Source: Schools Health Education Unit

but it's hard to fit it all in. Pupils studying business studies or economics learn something about inflation and interest rates, but the others don't.'

In a bid to boost personal finance knowledge at his school, Woodhead recently organised a one-day course for all 170 sixth-formers, with PFEG's help. He says: 'We looked at the costs of going to university, financing a gap year, consumer savvy, self-employment and managing your finance. We also held surgeries about pupils' finances.

'Quite a lot of students wanted to know about how to get the best deals when buying a mobile phone, or how to finance buying a car or pay for accommodation when they leave home.'

'Pupils studying business studies or economics learn something about inflation and interest rates, but the others don't'

Margaret Atherton of PFEG says: 'We help children under 16 look at different ways to buy things, taking in compound interest and different interest rates. Many teachers say they find the material personally helpful because they are learning things they themselves didn't know.

'Students are interested in personal budgeting and interest rates. They live in a cash economy and are slightly frightened of more sophisticated ways of managing their money. They are also concerned about higher education costs and indebtedness. Those going to university have little idea of the cost of living.

'They don't buy their own food or toothpaste or bleach and don't realise how much everything costs. Children from poorer homes can have an advantage because there's a lot of scrimping and saving and money is discussed at home. In better-off homes, parents may just hand over money and not talk about finances so their children tend to be less money-conscious.'

ProShare, launched 10 years ago to increase general understanding about stocks and shares, offers educational materials to secondary schools.

Tara Golshan of ProShare says: 'We have information packs about personal finance, banks, building societies and student loans, but our biggest educational project is the National Portfolio Challenge, which runs between October and February each year.'

Each team entering the competition selects and manages a £100,000 portfolio of 10 shares from different investment categories. They can trade when they wish, but must remember to deduct all stamp duty and trading costs. The most successful team wins a week's holiday in New York.

Last year, the winners beat both the FTSE100 index and a control portfolio suggested by investment advisers from HSBC who offered guidance to those taking part.

Younger children are asked to predict the share price of eight companies at a given date.

The Financial Services Authority will supply a range of educational materials, from play money and money-awareness exercises for junior schools to mock credit cards and cheques for older children who are unused to non-cash payment methods. It also offers personal finance modules for teenagers, covering areas such as risk assessment, ethical investments, e-commerce and insurance.

'Students live in a cash economy and are slightly frightened of more sophisticated ways of managing their money'

Various information leaflets are also available from the FSA on 020 7676 1000 or its website (www.fsa.gov.uk).

Education Extra is a charity that runs out-of-school maths clubs for young secondary school children in the South East of England. The aim is to help children master the basic financial skills they will need in adult life. Last week the charity received a £100,000 donation from Clerical Medical.

- FSA: 020 7676 1000
- PFEG: 020 7216 7550
- ProShare: 020 7720 1730

© *Telegraph Group Limited, London 2003*

Managing your debts

Information from the University of North London

Introduction

Debt nowadays is a common experience and occurs for a number of reasons, the most usual being:

- a sudden change of circumstances, such as relationship breakdown, illness or redundancy, leading to a dramatic fall in income,
- not being fully appraised of the financial implications of taking on something like a credit agreement,
- not enough money coming in in the first place.

Perhaps all three may apply to you but as a student the last one most certainly will. Whether you are experiencing a temporary shortage of cash, or reading these pages out of interest to help forestall a possible debt situation, or struggling with a multiplicity of debts and feel like you're sinking, then the following sections are for you.

Read the following information carefully and use it to help you get back in control of your finances.

Firstly, here's a reminder of some golden rules:

- Try not to ignore mounting debts or hide them – they don't go away.
- Never leave bills and bank statements unopened.
- Seek advice and help before the situation reaches crisis point.
- Maintain good relations with your bank.
- Realise most creditors are willing to talk to you about your problems and prepared to accept a realistic plan to repay the debt. Even if some are unhelpful don't give up trying to reach an agreement.
- Don't borrow money to pay off your debts – seek advice first.
- Resist the temptation to keep the more demanding, but lower priority, creditors happy by paying large amounts from your grant, student loan or other income. It will leave you without enough money for the real essentials such as food, rent, childcare costs, etc.

By Rachel Proudfoot

How to tackle your debts

There is no mystery about this. Standard money and debt advice comprises four basic steps:

1. Maximising your income.
2. Calculating your essential expenditure.
3. Sorting out your debts into priority order.
4. Negotiating with your creditors, and handling court papers and procedures if necessary.

Step (1): Maximising your income. Make sure that you have checked through all your entitlements and any other sources of income.

> *Realise most creditors are willing to talk to you about your problems and prepared to accept a realistic plan to repay the debt*

Step (2): Calculating your essential expenditure. By looking at your weekly or monthly budget plan you can work out your basic expenses plus any regular essential extra expenses i.e. all current bills. (Do not include the money you owe to your creditors as these are the debts you are planning to negotiate. Find out first how much you have left to offer them.)

* You must now try to maintain payments on all current essential expenditure to bring to a halt any future arrears on essential outgoings.

This step will help you prepare your Budget Sheet for Step (4) and work out realistic offers to your creditors. It will also help in planning future expenditure and can be reviewed as circumstances change.

Step (3): Sorting your debts into priority order. Debts are categorised as either priority or credit debts depending on the sanctions that can be applied. (NB Most debts owed to credit companies are in the latter category. Sanctions are more limited than those for priority debts, which is why more pressure may be applied to pay up.)

The following are classified as priority debts and they should be dealt with first to avoid loss of an essential amenity or facility. Listed against each debt is the ultimate sanction/s:

- Rent arrears – distraint/eviction
- Mortgage arrears (or any secured loan in arrears) – repossession/ eviction
- Water rates, gas and electricity arrears – disconnection
- Community Charge, Council Tax arrears, unpaid court fines – distraint/deduction from earnings (if you are employed) or Income Support or Job Seekers' Allowance/imprisonment. (For Council Tax imprisonment should not occur if the debtor genuinely can't pay.)
- Maintenance payments, Child Support payments arrears – as for Community Charge. (In the case of CSA debt the money can also be seized from a bank account.)
- Income tax, National Insurance, VAT arrears – distraint/bankruptcy
- Magistrates' Court fines e.g. not having a TV licence, driving offence – as for Community Charge
- Hire purchase arrears – repossession of goods

NB distraint = the ability of the creditor to send in a bailiff to remove and sell goods to cover the debt.

Others

Benefit overpayments – deductions from benefit (not Child Benefit) otherwise a credit debt.

Grant overpayments – deductions from future payments/court action.

Debts to the University may result in exclusion. If you get into difficulties or find you cannot meet the commitment to pay the tuition fees, hall fees, nursery fees, etc. then contact the relevant department without delay. If debts remain unpaid this may ultimately lead to exclusion from the University.

Emergency situation

Sometimes a debt can reach crisis point but check first to see what stage the sanctions procedure has actually reached before seeking further advice. It is important to have all the relevant documentation e.g. bills, letters, court summonses to hand.

Step (4): Negotiating with creditors, and handling court papers

Priority debts

Write a letter to these creditors first (or, if the situation is urgent, telephone and follow up with a letter confirming the call and any agreement reached) setting out how much you can offer. Don't worry if the amount offered appears very small if that's all you can afford. To aid your negotiations enclose your Budget Sheet which will show your financial position. Any arrangement will have to cover the current payment due plus something towards the arrears. A small regular payment is better than nothing, and better than making an arrangement you will not be able to keep.

Once negotiations are completed add these weekly figures to your Budget Sheet and see what's left over for the credit debts. Keep copies of any letters you send and file creditors' letters.

Credit debts

If there is any money left over you now prepare a Financial Statement to send to all these creditors (i.e. any not included above) listing:

If you have received a summons, or summonses, complete the papers as soon as possible

a) your weekly/monthly income
b) weekly/monthly expenditure
c) list of secondary creditors, the amounts owed and what you can offer them in proportion to what's owed – a pro-rata distribution. This is on the assumption that interest is frozen and this is something you will need to negotiate with these particular creditors.

This puts them all in the picture as to your financial situation.

Note: check first whether you are solely responsible for the debt if the agreement is in someone else's name or if you have taken it out jointly with another person.

Court and summonses

Should things reach this stage you are advised to get advice – see further sources of information and help.

Note: if you have received a summons, or summonses, complete the papers as soon as possible. Don't ignore them. Let the court have all the facts and supply a copy of your financial statement. Attend court hearings and bring a friend along for support. Take full details of your financial circumstances with you (other debts owed/demands, income, bank statements).

The court will send you its decision on how much is to be paid and in what instalments. If you fall behind on this, the creditor can arrange to seize your goods (or may take other action). If your circumstances change, you can apply to the court to renegotiate instalments.

County Court judgments for debt can affect future credit.

This is an outline of the steps you can take to bring debts back under control. Bear in mind it is not a quick fix or instant solution but a process whereby you can reach a position of financial viability which won't fall apart after a couple of weeks.

You will probably have to be honest with yourself and acknowledge some home truths about your spending habits but you don't have to beat yourself up!

Further sources of information and help

- National Debtline tel: 0808 808 4000 – expert advice over the telephone. They can also send you a free self-help pack *Dealing with Your Debts* which gives lots more information as well as telling you how to prepare a Budget Sheet or Personal Budget and a Financial Statement. They also have useful Fact Sheets free to individuals on e.g. Sample Letters to Creditors, Credit Reference Agencies, Bailiffs and the Council Tax, etc.
- Student Debt Helpline tel: 0800 328 1813 (8am – 8pm Monday – Friday). Free advice from the Consumer Credit Counselling Service
- Citizens' Advice Bureaux – details of all London Bureaus on Advice and Information Service's web pages
- UK Insolvency Helpline – independent debt and credit management advice
- Advice and Information Service – more detailed financial information and advice and also details of how to use this service at www.unl.ac.uk/ss/advice/
- The Student Services Centre in Tower Building keep a reference copy of *Dealing with Your Debts*.

© University of North London

'Avoid credit card debt', students warned

Consumer rights campaigners today warned students to avoid being seduced into applying for a credit card because of 'gimmicks' such as free cameras and book tokens.

Expensive credit card debt could 'push students over the edge', claimed the National Consumer Council (NCC) in advice timed to coincide with this year's freshers' week.

NCC chief executive Ed Mayo said credit cards were not the answer for cash-strapped undergraduates, and his warning was endorsed by the National Union of Students (NUS).

'Taking on credit card debt could push today's already indebted students over the edge'

Surveys have suggested that graduates can expect to finish university with a student loan, overdraft and other debts totalling between £10,000 and £15,000.

Tim, a computer science student at Aston University, said: 'When I arrived at my freshers' fair last year, we were all pressed by Barclaycard

By the Press Association

into applying for credit cards with the offer of free cameras or popcorn makers.

'The funny thing was I was not interested, but at the same time felt tempted. I got the popcorn maker but lucky for me I decided the card was too risky so I cut it up. I would advise other students to do the same.'

NUS president Mandy Telford confirmed the NUS's position. 'Don't be sucked in by free promotional offers when you open a credit card account,' she said. 'Make sure you read the small print and fully understand the charges that come with credit cards.'

'Taking on credit card debt could push today's already indebted students over the edge,' said Mr Mayo. 'The first lesson for students is that credit cards are not the answer. These free gifts are nothing but seductive offers to be ignored.'

A spokeswoman for APACS, the credit card industry's representative body, said it was developing a box that would go on promotional leaflets highlighting the features of each one. This will enable people to compare interest rates, charges and restrictions, as well as any special features such as free gifts, she said.

A spokesman for Barclaycard accused the NCC of insulting students' intelligence. 'We would never go in there and sell credit cards purely on the back of free cameras or other incentives, but the fact is that people like and appreciate these incentives,' he said.

■ This article first appeared in *The Guardian*, 18 September 2003.

© *The Press Association*

In a degree of debt

By Rami Okasha

So you want to be a student? Good decision. Both further and higher education increase your likelihood of gaining employment, getting promotion and getting paid a salary of or above the national average.

However, unless you are very lucky, you will not be rich as a student. In fact, students are given less money by the government than someone unemployed and on benefits. But with a bit of forward planning and careful budgeting, it is possible to avoid starvation. And if you can struggle through four years of cheap accommodation and baked beans, your earning power will increase for the rest of your life.

The first thing to remember is that a Scottish student studying in Scotland does not have to pay tuition fees – but you must fill out a lengthy Student Awards Agency for Scotland (SAAS) form. Every year, NUS Scotland deals with cases of students who, not having filled out the form, become liable to pay their own fees.

As a student, the Scottish Executive will give you an amount of money to live on. For most people, this is about £4,000. It will be made up of a loan, which you must pay back after your course, and bursary, which is like a grant. Exactly what proportion will be loan and what proportion bursary depends on your circumstances but, as a rule of thumb, you will not get any bursary if your parents earn more than £27,000. No matter what your circumstances, the total amount will stay the same – except for students whose parents earn less than £15,000, who will be loaned an extra £500, and students living at home, who get less.

Mature students and those who are self-supporting are not eligible for a bursary, but are entitled to apply to their university for money from the Mature Students' Bursary Fund after they have started the course. Students with children will be entitled to significant monies in the form of tax credits and a dedicated childcare grant.

When you fill out the SAAS form – available from www.saas.gov.uk – then the precise amount will be worked out for you based on the information you supply.

You won't have to start repaying your loan until after you graduate and once you start earning more than £10,000. As a Scottish student at a Scottish university, you will also have to pay a graduate endowment of £2,030. You can pay this in cash on the day you graduate, or you can extend your student loan to cover the payment. Some categories of students are exempt, so it is worth checking in advance.

> *The first thing to remember is that a Scottish student studying in Scotland does not have to pay tuition fees*

As a student, you will need to open a bank account, and will be presented with a bewildering array of high-street choices. The trick is to ignore the gimmicks: free teddy bears and CD vouchers might seem nice in freshers' week but will be useless a few months later when what you really need is a large overdraft. Most banks have special student accounts that entitle you to interest-free overdrafts. You should also get a Switch card and a chequebook – cheques are important for paying things such as rent, where you may need evidence of payment.

Credit cards cut both ways: they can be great for paying for food while you wait for the next instalment of money to clear, but if you don't pay bills off promptly you can end up paying hundreds of pounds in interest.

If at any point during the year, you run into financial difficulty, the worst thing you can do is ignore it. Debt won't go away, but you can manage it. For example, you will be able to apply for hardship funds: millions of pounds each year are given to universities and colleges for students who face immediate difficulty. You can expect to get between £200 and £1,000 in the case of genuine hardship. Forms are available from the students' association and from the university offices.

There will be tough times ahead, and you will accumulate debt. But few people who have had the privilege of being a student regret it.

Just the job

For most students, getting a part-time job is inevitable. The trick is to get one that pays well and doesn't interfere with your course too much. The summer break is when you will make most of your money, so start looking for summer jobs at Easter, but term-time jobs are necessary too.

Bar jobs do not sit easily with academic study. If you come home from a shift at 1am, you will have difficulty functioning at a 9am lecture. University libraries and admissions offices often employ students to stack shelves or show applicants around the campus.

Promotional work such as flyering and surveying people is also flexible, and can pay reasonably well.

Your university or student union is likely to have a jobshop; employers who advertise there clearly hire students. The local job centre will also have a large number of part-time jobs.

Remember your rights at work: you are entitled to breaks, holidays, a workplace free from discrimination and the minimum wage (from next month this is £3.80 for those aged 18-21; £4.50 for those over). And join a trade union immediately.

NUS/TUC student website: www.troubleatwork.org.uk

© 2003 The Scotsman

Thinking about university?

Information from Credit Action and the Shrievalty Association

Going to university should be one of the most exciting opportunities you get, but an increasing number of people are being put off because of:

- the cost;
- the need to take out a student loan; and
- the debt they will have to clear after they graduate.

If these things worry you, please remember that:

- people who don't go to university can end up in debt too;
- the debt need not be as bad as you think (you don't have to believe everything you read in the newspapers!); and
- the secret is to manage your money wisely – but it's not really a secret, just common sense.

A lot of people get hurt in motor accidents each year but that shouldn't stop you from driving a car. You just need to be careful. It's the same with the debt you get into as a student – you just need to be careful. With some careful planning and a bit of self-discipline, you can really cut down on the amount you need to borrow.

The cost of university

At today's prices, it costs about £7,500 to go to university for a year (add an extra £1,000 for a university in London). You need to allow for:

- tuition fees;
- course expenses such as books;
- living costs like accommodation, food, clothes and travel; and
- leisure activities.

All these costs must be met by:

- you – you can take out a loan which you will later have to repay;
- your parents – they are expected to pay something towards your fees if their income is above a certain level; and
- the Government – which funds student loans.

The money you contribute will come from a variety of sources such as your savings, a student loan, bank overdrafts and other forms of credit. This information will help you make up your mind about going to university by explaining the likely costs and where the money could come from.

Parents

You need to talk with your parents to find out how they are going to help pay for your time at university. If your parents cannot give you money, there are alternatives. What is important is that you know what you can expect. Will they pay a regular amount each month into your bank account? What would they do if you got into real financial difficulty? (Remember, most people today have money problems from time to time.)

Student loans

Most students take a loan from the Student Loans Company: the interest rates are low and you only start to repay when you have left university

---

You need to talk with your parents to find out how they are going to help pay for your time at university

---

and your income rises above a certain level. It is your decision whether you take out a student loan and, if so, how much you borrow (up to the maximum). In practice, most students need to take the full amount – but don't take it unless you need to.

Student loans are available if you are starting a full-time or sandwich course at a university or other publicly-funded college or at an NHS institution. Your course must lead to:

- a degree;
- a Diploma of Higher Education;
- a Higher National Diploma;
- a Postgraduate Certificate in Education (PGCE); or
- an equivalent qualification.

To be able to get a student loan, you normally:

- have to have lived in the UK for at least three years before the start of the course; and
- be aged under 50.

There are some exceptions, however, so it is always worth checking with your LEA (Local Education Authority).

Please remember the following when you are deciding whether you will take out a student loan:

- You can only apply for a loan twice in each academic year and for only one course at a time.

- The maximum amount you can get depends on where you live and study. You can get this information from your LEA.
- You do not have to take out a loan, but if you are eligible, you can borrow any amount up to your maximum. (This figure is lower in your final year because it does not take into account that year's summer holiday.)
- Loans are now subject to a 25% means test. This means you will receive 75% of your loan but your parents' income will be taken into account to see how much of the remaining 25% you are entitled to (unless you are financially independent).

Student debt

Many graduates are now leaving university with debts of well over £10,000 and this amount is likely to increase in the coming years. You start repaying the loan in the April after you graduate and, at the present rate, repay 9% of any income you receive each year over £10,000. This figure is expected to rise to £15,000 in 2005.

Your employer under the PAYE (Pay As You Earn) scheme usually takes your repayments direct from your salary (like tax). You can make extra voluntary payments at any time.

If you die, the loan is automatically paid off. If you never earn above the minimum threshold (currently £10,000), you will never have to repay your loan. But under the Government's present plans, if you go bankrupt you will still have to pay off your student loan.

Grants

From September 2004, students whose families earn less than £20,000 each year will be able to get grants of up to £1,000.

Tuition fees

Universities charge for teaching you – these are called tuition fees. You, your parents or your LEA have to pay a contribution towards these.

You can get help with these fees if you have lived in the UK for at least three years before starting your course. The amount you pay will be means tested, which means that your income and your parents' income are taken into account. There is a maximum amount you will have to pay – for the year 2003/2004 it is £1,125, but it is likely to rise in future years.

Other credit

More and more students find they have to borrow money on top of their student loan. Banks and other lenders want to lend students money in the hope they can keep their custom after they graduate. There are some good offers available but you must shop around.

You should be able to get a loan with 0% APR (no interest to pay) that will continue for up to a year after you graduate. You do not want to be hit by high interest rates immediately you leave university, especially if it takes a little while for you to find a job.

Your bank or building society will often increase your credit limit just because you ask . . . the golden rule is: don't borrow what you can do without

---

Do remember that if you ask, your bank or building society will often increase your credit limit just because you ask. This may seem very convenient but remember, the more you borrow the more you will have to pay back! The golden rule is: don't borrow what you can do without.

University access funds

All universities keep money aside (called access funds) for helping students who cannot make ends meet, particularly students with a low income. These funds are looked after by the student support office and usually are given out as grants (that is, you don't have to repay them). You will need to prove that you are struggling financially and that you have already got your maximum student loan.

If you find yourself in financial difficulty at university, always go to the student support office because even if they cannot help you, they should be able to refer you to someone who can.

Benefits for students

Full-time students cannot get Unemployment Benefit, Income Support or Housing Benefit: this applies during vacations as well. Some students, however, can claim benefits if they are:
- a single parent; or
- a disabled student who qualifies for the disability or severe disability premium (or who qualifies for a supplementary grant within the disability allowance because of deafness).

You will not pay Council Tax if you live in university accommodation or in a house where only full-time students live. (If a student lives with one adult who is not a student, that person can claim a 25% discount on their Council Tax bill.)

The future

The Government is considering changing both the way student loans work and the amount of tuition fees that universities can charge. You can get the latest information from your LEA and the Student Loans Company.

Student Loans Company Limited, 100 Bothwell Street, Glasgow, G2 7JD. Freephone 0800 405010. Website: www.slc.co.uk

Acknowledgements

This article has used information taken from the other Better Money Management Guides produced by Credit Action. Many people have helped, among them Stephen Rees (High Sheriff of Dyfed 2002/03), Margaret Royle (Surrey Education Business Partnership) and the staff and pupils of Glan-y-môr Ysgol at Bury Port. We are grateful to Barclays Bank plc, Cattles plc, members of the Shrievalty Association and supporters of Credit Action for their support in the production of this information. The authors are particularly grateful to the Plain English Campaign for numerous clarifications and simplifications to the text.

© 2003 Credit Action and the Shrievalty Association

KEY FACTS

■ It is estimated that an average student will expect to owe anything from £7,000 to £10,000 by the time they have completed their university studies. (p. 01)

■ Less than a fifth of 18- to 24-year-olds who are working say they are members of an occupational scheme and only one in 50, or 2 per cent, have a personal pension plan. (p. 01)

■ 'A 23-year-old saving £50 a month would have a pension pot of £100,000 which, on current rates will buy a pension of just £7,500 a year at the age of 65. (p. 02)

■ Two-thirds of the problems younger people have with debt is related to credit cards, store cards, overdrafts, loans and other sorts of easy credit. (p. 03)

■ The average tweenager received £7.02 a week last year, including pocket money and extras. This was up dramatically from £4.02 a week in 1997. (p. 04)

■ Sixty-two per cent of parents have given their children piggy banks and 46% have set up bank accounts for their children. However, 59% of parents thought schools taught just a little or nothing at all about money matters. (p. 06)

■ Many children take on part-time jobs. The Halifax found that nearly one in four 11 to 16-year-olds have a part-time job earning, on average, £27.31 a week. (p. 06)

■ There are two billion credit cards on high streets across the globe: they're part of our culture. (p. 09)

■ Britain is now spending more on plastic than cash and cheques and there are more than 60 different issuers, from banks and building societies to football clubs, offering a bewildering array of 1,500 different cards. (p. 09)

■ Lessons in personal finance have been part of the national curriculum for more than three years. (p. 12)

■ Borrowing, excluding mortgage debt, has never been higher. The figure has now topped £150 billion, according to the Bank of England. (p. 12)

■ The government wants 50% of young people to be in higher education by 2010. (p. 20)

■ While an eight-hour day is normal in the workplace, for many students it's just the start: 56% put in up to 20 hours of paid work a week on top of their education. (p. 20)

■ Depending on your year of study, the overdraft limit is usually between £750 and £2,000 (it grows as your student debts accumulate). (p. 21)

■ If you buy a TV for £100 and the company charges you 15% interest over one year, you will end up paying £115 in total. (p. 24)

■ If you have problem with debt, you're far from alone; Citizens' Advice Bureaux deal with over a million cases a year. They, the Consumer Credit Counselling Service (CCCS) and National Debt Line all dispense free advice. (p. 25)

■ Some store cards can charge you interest rates of around 30% a year. (p. 26)

■ Store cards are big business. There are 21 million in issue, compared with 8 million 10 years ago. (p. 27)

■ While the standard annual percentage rate (APR) on most store cards is about 30 per cent, you can pay around seven per cent on a personal loan, and many ordinary credit cards charge standard rates as low as 10 per cent. (p. 27)

■ Many college student services and/or students' union welfare services offer money management and debt counselling services. (p. 28)

■ The NUS Student Hardship Survey (1999) found that 41% of full-time undergraduates sampled undertook paid work during periods of study. The average hours of work were 13 per week and average pay was £4.53 per hour. (p.29)

■ A dedicated helpline for students worried about debt and money problems has been set up by the UK's leading debt charity, the Consumer Credit Counselling Service (CCCS). (p. 31)

■ Fewer than two in five consumers are confident about making their own financial decisions and only one in three has a clear idea of what financial products they need. (p. 32)

■ National Debtline tel: 0808 808 4000 – expert advice over the telephone. They can also send you a free self-help pack Dealing with Your Debts which gives lots more information as well as telling you how to prepare a Budget Sheet or Personal Budget and a Financial Statement. (p. 35)

■ Surveys have suggested that graduates can expect to finish university with a student loan, overdraft and other debts totalling between £10,000 and £15,000. (p. 36)

■ At today's prices, it costs about £7,500 to go to university for a year (add an extra £1,000 for a university in London). (p. 38)

ADDITIONAL RESOURCES

You might like to contact the following organisations for further information. Due to the increasing cost of postage, many organisations cannot respond to enquiries unless they receive a stamped, addressed envelope.

Consumer Credit Counselling Service
Wade House
Merrion Centre
Leeds, LS2 8NG
Tel: 0113 297 0121
E-mail: info@cccs.co.uk
Web site: www.cccs.co.uk
Consumer Credit Counselling Service (CCCS) is a registered charity whose purpose is to assist families and individuals who are in financial difficulty by providing independent and confidential counselling on personal budgeting, advice on the wise use of credit and, where appropriate, achievable plans to repay outstanding debts. For free, confidential debt advice call 0800 138 1111.

Credit Action
6 Regent Terrace
Cambridge, CB2 1AA
Tel: 01223 324034
Fax: 01223 324034
E-mail: office@creditaction.com
Web site: www.creditaction.com
and www.debtcred.org.uk
Promotes self-help in personal money matters. Credit Action helpline 0800 591054.

Credit Card Research Group
2 Ridgmount Street
London, WC1E 7AA
Tel: 020 7436 9937
Fax: 020 7580 0016
Web site:
www.plasticmoney.org.uk and
www.ccrg.org.uk
The Credit Card Research Group informs, lobbies and promotes the credit and debit card industry to the media, Government and consumer groups.

Lifetime Careers Publishing
7 Ascot Court
White Horse Business Part
Trowbridge
Wiltshire, BA14 0XA
Tel: 01225 716027
Fax: 01225 716025
Web site: www.lifetime-
publishing.co.uk

National Federation of Women's
Institutes
104 New Kings Road
London, SW6 4LY
Tel: 020 7371 9300
Fax: 020 7736 3652
E-mail: hq@nfwi.org.uk
Web site: www.womens-
institute.co.uk
Publishes the magazine Woman's
World.

National Union of Students (NUS)
Nelson Mandela House
461 Holloway Road
London, N7 6LJ
Tel: 020 7272 8900
Fax: 020 7263 5713
E-mail: nusuk@nus.org.uk
Web site: www.nusonline.co.uk
Represents the students of the UK locally, nationally and internationally and to promote their interests.

National Youth Agency (NYA)
17-23 Albion Street
Leicester, LE1 6GD
Tel: 0116 285 3700
Fax: 0116 285 3777
E-mail: nya@nya.org.uk
Web site: www.nya.org.uk
The National Youth Agency aims to advance youth work to promote young people's personal and social development, and their voice, influence and place in society.

0-19 Magazine
Reed Business Information Limited
6th floor
Quadrant House, The Quadrant
Sutton, SM2 5AS
Tel: 020 8652 3500
Fax: 020 8652 4739
Web site:
www.zero2nineteen.co.uk
0-19 is for all professionals working to help children and young people at risk of social exclusion to make the most of their lives and opportunities.

The Push Guides
Southbank House
Black Prince Road
London, SE1 7SJ
Tel: 020 7463 0655
E-mail: webteam@push.co.uk
Web site: www.push.co.uk
No-one can tell you the truth about university like someone who's living it.

INDEX

insurance, and young people 2, 15
interest rates
    and credit 23
    credit cards 26, 27
    and savings 24
    and the Student Loans Company 38
Internet banking, and young people 2

LEAs (local education authorities), and student loans 38
lone parents, students 39

married couples, and financial decision-making 6
money matters
    and the cashless society 9-11
    and children 4, 5-6, 6-7, 12-13
    financial planning 14-39
    public attitudes to 5-6
    students 1, 17, 19-22, 28-32, 34-9
    teenagers 8-9
    will making 16
    see also banks

National Youth Agency 17
NCC (National Consumer Council), and credit card
    debt 36
Nestlé family monitor, *Money in the Contemporary
    Family* 5-6
numeracy skills, of adults in Britain 32
NUS (National Union of Students) 28-30, 31
    and credit cards 36

parents
    and money matters
        savings 7
        teaching children about 1, 5-6
    and student money management 19, 38
part-time jobs
    children and teenagers with 6, 8, 9
    students with 20, 37
pension planning, and young people 1-2
PFEG (Personal Finance Education Group) 12, 13, 32-3
pocket money 6, 8, 9, 13, 14
ProShare 33
public attitudes, to money matters 5-6

savings
    attitudes to 5
        children 6-7
    and parents 7
    savings accounts
        for children 13
        and young people 19, 24
    and teenagers 8-9
    and young people 15
schools, teaching about money matters 1, 6, 12, 32-3
Scotland, abolition of tuition fees in 20, 37
shopping
    and budgeting 23
    and money management 17
State benefits
    Child Benefit 7

Children's Tax Credit 7
    and students 39
    Working Families Tax Credit 7
store cards 27
students
    and money matters 1, 17, 19-22, 28-32, 34-9
        bank accounts 1, 2, 17, 21-2, 29, 32
        bank loans 39
        budgeting 2, 28, 30, 32
        bursaries 32, 37
        costs of a university education 38
        course costs 30
        credit cards 3, 30, 32, 36, 37
        and debts 1, 3, 5, 19-20, 28-9, 31-2, 34-9
        disabled students 39
        estimated average student expenditure 29
        graduate starting salaries 31
        grants 39
        hardship funds 37
        living at home 19
        living and study costs 28, 30
        mature students 37
        money management support services 28
        overdrafts 1, 21-2, 37
        and paid employment 20, 29, 37
        and parents 19, 38
        record keeping 28
        single parents 39
        and state benefits 39
        statutory support 29
        Student Loans Company 5, 38-9
        tuition fees 19, 20, 31, 37, 39
        understanding your entitlements 28
        university access funds 39
    in Scotland 20, 37
    see also universities

teenagers see young people
tweenagers, and money matters 4

universities
    costs of a university education 38
    funding higher education 19-20
    see also students

wages, for students 37
will making 16

young people
    and money matters 1-4, 14-17
        attitudes to money 2
        budgeting 2, 3, 14-15, 23
        credit cards 15, 16
        debt 1, 2, 15, 16, 23-4
        and insurance 2, 15
        paying bills 2
        pension planning 1-2
        savings 15
        teenagers 8-9
        tweenagers 4
    see also students

ACKNOWLEDGEMENTS

The publisher is grateful for permission to reproduce the following material.

While every care has been taken to trace and acknowledge copyright, the publisher tenders its apology for any accidental infringement or where copyright has proved untraceable. The publisher would be pleased to come to a suitable arrangement in any such case with the rightful owner.

Chapter One: Personal Finances
Catching them young, © Woman's World, *A generation unskilled in the art of budgeting*, © Telegraph Group Limited, London 2003, *Being taught about money matters*, © Nestlé Family Monitor/MORI, *£1bn power of the tweenagers*, © The Daily Mail, January 2003, *Study shows debt as a recipe for family friction*, © 2003 MORI, *Saving money*, © Nestlé Family Monitor/MORI, *You're never too young to spend, spend, spend*, © Guardian Newspapers Limited 2003, *Spending money*, © Halifax Pocket Money Survey 2003, *Cash in hand*, © 0-19 Magazine, *Money – earning it*, © NCH, *Is a cashless society on the cards?*, © Trinity Mirror plc, *The moneywise generation*, © Associated Newspapers Ltd, *What schools should teach about financial matters*, © Nestlé Family Monitor/MORI, *Vital lessons*, © Associated Newspapers Ltd.

Chapter Two: Money Management
You and your money, © Lifetime Careers Wiltshire Ltd, *Saving money*, © Schools Health Education United (SHEU), *Managing your own bank account*, © National Youth Agency, *Banking*, © Barclays Bank Plc 2003, *Earn as you learn?*, © John Crace, *Student debt*, © National Union of Students (NUS), *Banks*, © Push 2003, *Managing money*, © Barclays Bank Plc 2003, *Ten tips for cutting debt*, © Guardian Newspapers Limited, *Credit cards*, © Credit Card Research Group, *Storing up trouble*, © Telegraph Group Limited, London 2003, *Managing your money*, © National Union of Students (NUS), *Student expenditure*, © National Union of Students (NUS), *Student debt*, © Consumer Credit Counselling Service, *Student loan scheme*, © Nestlé Family Monitor/ MORI, *'There is a real need to upgrade financial literacy'*, © Telegraph Group Limited, London 2003, *Items bought in the last week*, © Schools Health Education United (SHEU), *Managing your debts*, © University of North London, *'Avoid credit card debt', students warned*, © The Press Association, *In a degree of debt*, © 2003 The Scotsman, *Thinking of university?*, © 2003 Credit Action and the Shrievalty Association.

Photographs and illustrations:
Pages 1, 10, 21, 28: Pumpkin House; pages 4, 17, 20, 24, 30, 36, 38: Simon Kneebone; pages 14, 18, 25, 26; Bev Aisbett.

Craig Donnellan
Cambridge
January, 2004